Fishing the Rivers of the Mid-Atlantic

Fishing the Rivers of the Mid-Atlantic

by Bill Anderson

Tidewater Publishers
Centreville, Maryland

Library of Congress Cataloging-in-Publication Data

Anderson, Bill
    Fishing the rivers of the Mid-Atlantic / by Bill Anderson. — 1st
ed.
        p.   cm.
    ISBN 0-87033-413-1 (pbk.) :
    1. Fishing—Middle Atlantic States.   2. Fishing—Middle Atlantic
States—Guide-books.   3. Rivers—Middle Atlantic States—Guide
-books.   4. Middle Atlantic States—Description and travel—Guide
-books.   I. Title.
SH464.M53A53 1991
799.1′1′0974—dc20   90-50372
                                                            CIP

The maps of the rivers were drawn by A. L. Wilson. All photos are by the author unless otherwise noted.

Manufactured in the United States of America
First edition

Contents

Foreword

The great limestone rivers of the mid-Atlantic area offer some of the best light tackle fishing anywhere on this continent—and certainly some of the top smallmouth action. There are a number of these rivers: the Potomac, New, Shenandoah, Susquehanna, James, Juniata, and more. How do you find and then fish these waters? What kind of boats and tackle are needed? And are there poor, good, and best times or seasons to fish them?

There has been a definite need for a book that answers all these questions—and more. And, even if you thoroughly understand your local river, there is always a promise and joy to fishing another of these great waterways.

Bill Anderson, whom I have fished with often on some of these waters, is well qualified to do such a book. He is a fine writer/reporter as well as an accomplished angler. The combination has enabled him to produce a work that will benefit anyone who wants to catch more fish in these rivers.

How largemouth and smallmouth bass differ—in habitat, the types of tackle and lures they rise to, and even methods of fishing for them—is well covered. Bill also teaches the reader how to catch big catfish, muskie, carp, and panfish. In short, if you don't know what kinds of lures, baits, or flies to use, this book will help you.

Two of the best features of the book are the detailed listings of public boat ramps and the superb maps that illustrate the different rivers. They alone are well worth the price.

This book is by a man who has waded, floated, and boated all of these waters. This is a book written for serious fishermen by a serious angler.

Lefty Kreh

Preface

This book is a compilation of facts and figures, the product of several years of research. Like most books, this one started with an idea: After the publication of one of my magazine articles on the Potomac River, which included a map and some detailed information on access points and float trip possibilities, I was so overwhelmed by the favorable response that I mentioned to Lefty Kreh that someone should do a book on the whole river, a complete account of such information.

As usual, Lefty was able to see the bigger picture and suggested that what was needed was a book, not just on the Potomac, but including some of the other similar rivers of the region. He noted that such a book would certainly fill a niche in the angling world.

The culmination of my efforts you now hold in your hand. Most of the information you will find herein is a result of talking with people from the various regions: officials from the different state agencies, fellow newspaper writers, and fishermen. Every possible effort has been made to bring you accurate, up-to-date information on the rivers and the public facilities such as boat ramps. But bear in mind that such data change from year to year. New ramps are added, and in some cases others may be closed. The editors and I also made the decision to go strictly with public facilities; however, on some rivers you may find private facilities available that will suit your needs for access to the rivers.

You should also note that this is not the complete book on every mile of every river. I tried to make it that early on and discovered that I probably wouldn't live long enough to complete such a project. Consider this an overview, if you will, of each river, and a fairly complete one. Anglers armed with this book should be able to journey to the rivers and find the kinds of water conditions and access facilities that will enable them to enjoy fishing selected sections of the rivers.

You will see that I have completely omitted, or warned against, certain sections of certain rivers. The Gorge section of the New River comes to mind as a place that fishermen should avoid. This is a book on fishing, not whitewater boating. Most fishermen aren't skilled whitewater boaters, and it's been my experience that most whitewater enthusiasts aren't really into fishing.

Although I've made a conscious effort to warn you of unusually dangerous waters, neither myself nor the publisher assumes any responsibility for your safety when you do approach the rivers. In 1988, a very rainy year, eighteen people drowned on the upper Potomac—and the Potomac is one of the gentlest rivers of the lot. The point is that any of these rivers is capable of taking a life if the angler is careless, or fails to show proper respect. Some rivers are far more dangerous than others, but each can be dangerous under certain conditions, such as high waters after periods of rain.

In closing, I have many to thank for their assistance in completing this project. First, the fisheries biologists in the different states who provided many of the data for the book. Without their help it would have been impossible to complete a work such as this. And without their hard work, under trying conditions, we really wouldn't have a worthwhile subject on which to base this book. From Pennsylvania: Larry Jackson and Dick Snyder of the Pennsylvania Fish Commission. From Maryland: Ed Enamait and Bob Bachman of the Maryland Department of Natural Resources. From West Virginia: Gerald Lewis and Jim Reed of the West Virginia Department of Natural Resources. And from Virginia: Larry Mohen and David Whitehurst of the Virginia Department of Game and Inland Fisheries.

I would also like to thank fellow outdoors writers who contributed photos and invaluable information: Bill Cochran, Gerald Almy, Mike Sawyers, and Lefty Kreh.

To Lefty Kreh I owe a special mention. Lefty more or less adopted me about ten years ago, and has always been there to offer advice, support, and encouragement. From Lefty I have learned much about fishing, hunting, natural science, and the business of outdoors writing. But most of all Lefty has become a special friend.

Two outstanding river fishermen also merit credit. Ed Lewis and Butch Ward have shared many of their secrets on river smallmouths and their help is greatly appreciated.

And last, but certainly not least, I would like to thank my dad, Kyle Anderson, for always making time to take a towheaded kid fishing on the Potomac.

Fishing the Rivers of the Mid-Atlantic

ONE

The River Fishing Experience

I grew up along a small tributary stream of the Potomac River in western Maryland. As a very small kid, I spent hours exploring the different sections of that stream, learning the various things that make river and stream fishing so engaging.

I learned, for example, that the frogs would most often be found living in the little weed beds in the slower pools, while the few remaining trout in the stream preferred the faster-moving waters, usually below riffles. I didn't know this at the time, but know now, that the trout were there because the riffled water contained the most oxygen during the summer months.

I learned which pools contained the large schools of minnows, and where the rock bass lived, and that the bigger fish were usually found in the deeper pools, especially those that also featured cover such as undercut banks for the fish to hide beneath.

Whenever my dad could spare the time, he would take me to the Potomac, where we would fish for channel catfish, smallmouth bass, and carp. And I found, when I viewed the river and tried to figure out why the fish were in certain spots, that the river was nothing more than a bigger model of the little stream I knew so well. The fish that lived in the river were different, but they were motivated by the same factors. They would seek out the habitat they were most comfortable in, and the areas they could find food and security in.

As a fisherman who uses outdoors writing as an excuse to fish many different types of water each season, from the brawling trout rivers of the West to the large impoundments in the East for largemouth bass and striped bass, I must admit to a special love for the rivers of the mid-Atlantic. Perhaps this is because of those early years along the tiny stream, but, whatever the reason, river fishing holds a special fascination for me.

I view each river as a special, almost alive, entity. Each has its own personality, and its own rewards. And, for the careless angler, each

3

*Nature study is part of the river ex-
perience—this great horned owl
was spotted during a fishing trip.*

river has its hazards that can claim a life in an instant if proper respect
isn't shown.

The fishing in each river is basically the same, yet, at the same
time, always different. In fact no two trips on one river can ever be
exactly identical in all ways. There will be differences in the water
temperature, water coloration, air temperature, and the many other
factors that provide a river fishing experience as challenging as you
choose to make it. The fish, and the fishing, will be influenced by those
variations and other factors that we still don't understand.

Striving to understand the rivers, and the fish that live therein, is
a continual learning experience.

SEASONS OF THE RIVERS

As I write this, it is late in December, and the fishing season is still
underway. My boys and I just returned from the Potomac, where I

dipped my thermometer into the river to find out if the water temperature had dropped below 40 degrees; if so, the season would be finally
over. But the water temperature was 43 degrees just before dark, and
tomorrow I will fish for smallmouth bass.

What a season it has been! The fishing began with an unusually
warm spell in February, and has lasted (with interruptions for high
water after rains) since that time. Not too many years ago, I stopped
fishing when the leaves turned in the fall, and spent my time with gun
or bow in hand, searching the fields and forests for grouse, or squirrels,
or deer. Now I know that some of the very best fishing of the year occurs
when most sportsmen are busy with the fall hunting seasons.

To be a river fisherman is to understand the seasonal moods of the
rivers—to know that, in the springtime, typical spring rains will often
make the rivers high and muddy, but also to know that, if you can get
there right after the rains, when the river is just beginning to rise, the
fishing is sometimes superb. It is to recognize which water temperatures the different species of gamefish prefer, and to be aware of when
the fish should begin to feed after a winter of fasting.

The river fisherman knows about spawning times, when the
gamefish will be preoccupied with procreation, and the types of habitat each species prefers. And each angler will make his or her own
decision on whether or not they feel comfortable going after fish that
are spawning.

It is in the summertime that most fishermen visit the rivers, and
the serious river fishermen know that in the summertime it is hard to
catch big river smallmouths on artificial lures—the best bet is to use
live bait.

But the summertime has its own rewards: wading the river
during a hot, humid evening, feeling the comforting waters around
your legs, and letting the river wash away the stresses of our hurried
lives.

If you are a fly fisherman, you will come to know that, on those hot
summer evenings, there will usually be hatches of mayflies or caddis
flies and the fish will rise to those flies, and to your imitations made of
fur and feather.

Summertime is the time for carefully planned float trips, which
offer the fisherman access to waters that ordinarily can't be reached by
boat or on foot. It's the time of year when the river creatures, such as
aquatic insects, crustaceans like the crayfish, and minnows, are at
peak populations, and the gamefish have a wide variety of forage to
choose from.

*Ed Dentry with a big smallmouth taken during an
early autumn float trip.*

Summertime is a great time to be on the rivers, but it is in the fall,
about the time that the best teams from the American League and the
National League square off in the American institution called the
World Series, that the fall fishing season begins, and the fishing enters
what I call the "Season of the Trophy Smallmouths."

Fall fishing is special for me, and one of my biggest regrets is all
the fine fishing I missed before I knew how productive fall fishing for
big river smallmouths can be.

Fall fishing has its own special charm and rewards, not the least of
which is the beauty of the rivers when the banks are lined with trees
sporting leaves colored scarlet and gold. The best fishing starts when
the nights turn chilly, and the ground is covered with frost when you
launch your boat in the morning fog. The fog will almost always be
there, a result of the cool air meeting the warmer water of the river.

Fishing season can last into the winter on the rivers. This big bass was taken during a November snow shower.

The fall smallmouth is a virile creature. The fish seem determined to make the most of the remaining nice weather and feed heavily to prepare for winter. Also, if you ever clean a mature female smallmouth in the fall, you will notice that she is full of eggs, and the heavy feeding in the fall helps in the development of the eggs she will deliver to a nest next spring.

The smallmouth fishing will last until the water temperature drops below 40 degrees. Many of the better fishermen on the Potomac prefer the temperature to be between 42 and 45 degrees for optimum results. In my area this usually means the fishing will last until late November or early December, and for some reason the best fishing is often during Thanksgiving week, which also happens to be the first week of the deer season in West Virginia. More than once, I've returned from a deer camp with an unfilled tag to find out that my friends have been enjoying the finest fishing of the season.

The fishing season doesn't have to end with the onset of winter, however. In the rivers with muskies and walleyes, hardy anglers fish right through the bitter weather, and often do quite well.

Another winter alternative is fishing below power plants that feature warm water discharges. On the Potomac River, for example, the

Dickerson power plant, near Frederick, Maryland, releases warm water into the river that allows for fishing on a year-round basis. On several occasions we have recorded as much as 15 degrees' difference in water temperature on the Maryland side of the river below the discharge (as opposed to the Virginia side). Anglers take channel catfish and smallmouth bass from the warm water during the coldest months of the year.

THE COMPLETE RIVER FISHING EXPERIENCE

There is more to river fishing than simply catching fish, or knowing what the best times of the year are, or what water temperatures are optimum for the different species.

The astute river fisherman will come to know all the creatures that make the waters and banks their home. Take a few moments to lift a rock, or run your hand through a weed bed to sample the wide variety of aquatic insects that live in the rivers. Learn how to identify the immature mayflies called nymphs, and the immature caddis flies called pupae. Learn the places the hellgramites live, and where the crayfish prefer to reside.

On almost every river outing you will see wildlife—song birds, deer, beaver, or majestic birds of prey. Two of my fondest memories are associated with raptors. The first involved seeing an immature bald eagle working the banks of the South Branch of the Potomac in West Virginia, and the other was the sight of a beautiful osprey diving into the river just yards from our boat on a Potomac float trip with my buddy Ed Dentry.

Other memories include watching a nimble mink eating a crayfish as we drifted by only a few feet from his dinner table, and watching a family of beavers bring in the winter's supply of groceries. Such experiences make the trip exciting, no matter the mood of the fish.

The rivers of the mid-Atlantic offer us almost unlimited outdoor recreational opportunities and, because of this, are one of our nation's most valuable natural resources. No matter if your interest is primarily fishing, boating, camping, or simply enjoying nature; the rivers, and the creatures that live in and near the rivers, are there for us all to enjoy. It is the responsibility of each and every one of us to make sure that the rivers remain at least as healthy as they are today—a haven for the river creatures and for the people who choose to enjoy them.

Over the years, the rivers have endured their share of man's abuse. But in almost every case, this trend has been stopped, and, in fact,

Beaver and their dams are common on most of the rivers.

reversed. The Potomac is a classic example. I can remember well the Potomac of the 1960s, filled with algae and actually declared unfit for swimming near Washington, D.C.

But the Potomac is now a river reclaimed and, over the past ten years, seems to get cleaner each year. Similar successes have occurred on other rivers. But, friends, always remember this: The people who control such matters are politicians and, as politicians, tend to reflect the mood of the people. During the 1960s and 1970s, environmental matters were given a high national priority and the rivers fared well. But if the mood of the people changes, the trend toward a cleaner environment can be reversed. Such priorities as energy production could change the agenda, and the progress made could be lost in only a few months.

It is therefore vitally important that those of us who love and respect nature continue the fight for a clean environment, and for protection of the rivers. For what good is cheap energy if there is no place for the river creatures to live?

TWO

Wading and Bank Fishing

When I was a barefoot boy roaming the banks of the Potomac, confined to fishing from the Maryland shore, I felt totally restricted in my options concerning which waters I could fish.

Later, after becoming more or less gainfully employed, and the owner of a boat and motor, I abandoned bank fishing, preferring the mobility of fishing from a boat. An episode with a Williamsport, Maryland, angler caused a change in my thinking.

The call was typical of those a newspaper writer receives: An angler had caught a big fish, and wondered if the paper would be interested in a picture. The angler was Robert Cunningham, and he had three big river smallmouths, all caught in one morning.

Usually the sports editor vetoed such "hero" shots, but I checked out the catch and found that the bass weighed, respectively, five pounds, two ounces; four pounds, nine ounces; and three pounds, twelve ounces. The fisherman had my attention.

Later, when we met for the photos, Robert explained that he had caught the bass in about an hour of fishing, and he even invited me to join him the next morning. Such invitations are unusual, since expert anglers seldom share their spots with strangers—particularly strangers who could blab the secret all over the Sunday sports section.

We hit the river just after daylight. As is often the case during Indian summer, a heavy fog shrouded the water. Robert explained that the fog was important. "It helps hide the fisherman from the fish," he said.

The bait was big chub minnows that Robert had caught in the river several days earlier, and the pool we were fishing—the spot that had produced the big stringer the previous day—was in a long flat on the river. Robert told me the water was only three to four feet deep.

Branches protruding through the surface showed that the area held sunken brush. Robert explained that the brush held minnows, and that the bass came to feed on the abundant forage.

10

Robert Cunningham with a stringer of big
river smallmouths taken from the shore.

Robert's approach to the fishing was decidedly simple. His rods were medium bait-casting models, and the reels were Zebco 33 spin-casting models. The reels were loaded with ten-pound-test mono, and he was fishing the big minnows without additional weight attached to the line.

As we rigged up, I could see swirls near the brush piles, which indicated that the bass were busy acquiring breakfast. Robert was the first to cast out, and within moments a few tentative taps indicated that a bass had found the bait. Robert let the bass run a few feet and then set the hook on a three-pound smallmouth. A few moments later an almost identical fish hit my minnow just after it touched the water, and I was able to land it.

We each picked up an additional fish before the sun came out and the fog started burning off the water. "This will probably be it for today," Robert said. "When the sun hits the water, the fish get spooky and move into deeper pools."

The point of all this is that, although Robert owned a boat and motor he could have been using, he felt sure that the hole would have

*Cunningham demonstrates his technique
the following day.*

been ruined by approaching it by boat. "The big smallmouths are real
spooky when the water is clear in the fall," he explained, "and the noise
that a boat makes would have put them out of the area."

Since that time I've talked with other successful anglers who feel
the same way. When the fish are in clear, shallow water—conditions
experienced in the early fall—it is very hard to approach them in an
aluminum boat without them knowing you are in the area.

Approaching a fishing spot from the shore can be used in many
areas, and, in fact, in some areas it is the only method to use because
the waters are too low to make boating practical.

In other areas I use a combination of approaching and fishing from
the shore, and also wading to reach spots too far out to be reached from
land.

Wading the rivers is a particularly pleasant experience for me, and
I am rejuvenated by letting the waters wash the problems of day-to-day
life away. During the summer months, you can simply wet-wade, with
an old pair of pants on and some shoes to protect your feet. As a kid, I
waded in sneakers, but now have found that the best footwear is a pair

Wading will often allow you to reach waters that others don't fish.

of wading shoes with felt soles that help me keep my footing on rocks that are often covered with greaselike algae.

Wading doesn't have to end when summer passes, because with chest-high wading boots or, in some cases, hip boots, you can fish the river right through the fall, which is often the best time to wade. Obviously, this applies only when the river is still at a low flow level, before the late autumn rains.

Another productive method in shallow water conditions is to use a canoe or shallow-draft johnboat to drift the river, and then get out and wade-fish the better pools and flats. This allows you to cover a large amount of water, while still enjoying the advantage of wading to approach spooky fish. Wielding a fly rod is much easier while wading than when in a boat, particularly a canoe.

Anglers should always remember that wading can be dangerous in certain rivers. I think particularly of the Potomac near Harpers Ferry and certain sections of the New River in West Virginia below Bluestone Reservoir; but all the rivers have areas that can fool you. The Harpers Ferry section of the Potomac is deceptive—it doesn't look deep, and certainly not dangerous. But the fast-moving waters and underwater rock formations create swirls, holes, and undercurrents that have claimed many lives over the years. In fact, unless you know a section of water very thoroughly, undertake all wading with extreme caution. Be sure to wear good wading shoes or boots, and you may want to carry a staff to help you maintain balance in fast current.

   The river fish are exciting, but there has never been a fish worth risking your life for.

THREE

Riverboats

Almost every river fisherman will have need of a boat of some type during the course of the fishing season. Even if you are one of the stealthy types who prefer to carefully approach potential hot spots by wading, there will be times when the water is too deep, or too cold, or both, and will require the use of a boat.

During my travels to the different rivers, I have noted boats of almost every size and description being used by fishermen. In some of the deepwater areas on the Potomac, you will often see big fiberglass bass boats, powered by outboards of up to 150 horsepower. However, such boats are for deepwater work only, and cannot be considered typical river fishing boats—at least in the nontidal sections of the rivers that we are concerned with.

The workhorse boat for the river fishermen is the flat-bottomed johnboat, the size of the boat primarily determined by the type of water the fisherman prefers fishing. The angler who usually makes float trips over shallow-water sections will often choose a light twelve-foot johnboat because of the ease of portability, while anglers who like to trailer their boat to a ramp and run from spot to spot usually like a larger boat. On the Potomac the regulars seem to prefer a fifteen- or sixteen-foot, flat-bottomed, aluminum boat.

THE CUSTOM RIVERBOAT

No matter the type of boat you choose as your riverboat, there are several modifications you can make that will turn a standard johnboat hull into a custom river fishing boat. As an example of some of the modifications that can be performed, I will use my own boat, which may not be ideal, but serves well for the type of fishing that I most often engage in.

Since I travel a lot, I needed a boat that could be trailered from spot to spot, yet large enough to work on small lakes and also in the rocky rivers of the mid-Atlantic.

Small johnboat is excellent for low water float trips.

After checking out several hull designs, I bought a Fisher Marine Model 15-V, which is 15 feet long and 39½ inches wide on the bottom, and features a slight vee in the bow to fight through a light chop on lakes.

The boat is powered by a fifteen-horsepower OMC outboard which allows the boat to plane at speeds of about fifteen miles per hour with two adults and their fishing gear aboard. The boat is large enough to allow fishermen to safely stand up when fishing and yet is still light enough to allow me to jump out and pull it through the shallow riffle areas that are common in the rivers of the mid-Atlantic.

Bolt-On Additions
Prop Guard
One of the most important additions to any river fishing boat is a guard to protect the prop from the many rocks and rock formations that make up the bottom of all these rivers.

One of the oldest prop guards is the head of a pitchfork strapped to the lower unit of the outboard—it protects the prop quite satisfactorily. However, several Maryland anglers used the basic design of the pitchfork guard to create a much more effective prop guard.

This guard is made from ⅜-inch-diameter stainless steel rod, and is bolted to the cavitation plate on the lower unit. One of the biggest problems with any prop guard is that it deflects water away from the prop, which causes a loss in performance, and, in some cases, cavitation. However, the design of the propeller guard is such that cavitation is only infrequently a problem; and while there is a loss in performance, the net advantages of the prop guard make it a worthwhile trade-off.

Rod Holders

On any given outing I will be carrying spinning tackle, bait-casting tackle, and fly-fishing tackle in my boat. This means that there will be four or more rods in the boat for my use, plus the rods my partner brought along.

Obviously, you can only use one rod at a time, so it makes sense to have a place to store the other rods while you are traveling, and while they are not in use. Most of the expensive rods I've broken were stepped on when they were carelessly placed on the floor of the boat.

You can buy completely satisfactory rod holders at most boating and tackle stores, or you can build your own to fit your individual needs and to custom-fit your boat. But do install rod holders—the rods you save will probably be your own.

Anchors and Anchor Releases

In many situations, an anchor will be needed to secure your boat so that you can thoroughly fish a given area or a particular spot. Almost anything can be used for an anchor, and over the years I've seen junk metal, pieces of cinder block, and even rocks pressed into service. Many river anglers use the mushroom-shaped anchors sold in most boating stores but, while they work satisfactorily in some situations, they aren't ideal for river use.

The anchor type I've found most useful for fishing the rocky rivers where current can be a factor is a wedge-shaped piece of poured lead that some river anglers call a mule anchor.

The shape of this anchor makes it ideal for river use because the flat side of the anchor will catch and hold on underwater rock formations when the anchor is dropped, yet it resists permanent hang-ups that often cause anglers to lose their anchors.

Homemade rod racks help protect expensive fishing rods.

I've never found a commercial source for the mule anchor, and everyone I know using the style makes them by forming up a mold and filling it with molten lead. My anchor weighs only six pounds and holds my fifteen-foot boat easily—even in a fairly heavy current.

An anchor release is a handy item to have on your boat, and you can go with the fancy releases that include a manual or even an electric winch to haul up the anchor when you are ready to move on. There are, however, simple manual releases that work just fine on riverboats (where you seldom have a great deal of anchor line out). The release I'm using costs less than ten dollars and releases line when you hold the line up, and clamps the line when you push down. The rollers on the release make lifting the anchor nearly effortless, far easier than pulling it up over the side of the boat without a release mechanism.

One important point on anchoring below a big hydroelectric dam such as Conowingo on the Susquehanna or Bluestone on the New River: When the operator of the facility decides to release water, the river level below the dam can rise at a rate that few would believe. If you are anchored, and your anchor becomes snagged, rising waters can soon use up the slack in the anchor line, causing the boat to be dragged under. It's a sad but important fact to report that this situation, with lives lost, has occurred over the years.

When fishing below such facilities, the fisherman should be alert for sirens that warn of impending water releases and take care to check anchors before the waters begin to reach a dangerous level. It is also important to have in your possession a sharp knife that will allow you to rid yourself of the anchor if it is hung and the waters are quickly rising.

Electronics

Most river fishermen probably feel that the modern electronics found on high-powered bass boats have no place in river fishing. For the most part they are right, but there are situations where a depth finder, or fish finder as they are sometimes called, can earn its keep on a riverboat.

River fishing, as we are discussing it, is basically shallow-water fishing, and you can usually see the bottom of the river. But in each river there are deepwater pools that have you wondering what kind of structure might be on the bottom to hold fish.

Most of my early sonar work on the Potomac was done with a flasher type unit that would scan the bottom; by reading the flashes of light on a scale you could find out what the bottom looked like. The skilled operator could even tell the difference between mud and rock, and which erratic pulses indicated submerged brush.

But the flasher type units have now been replaced with what are called LCD (liquid crystal display) units which, as a reflection of the computer industry, continue to get better, smaller, and less expensive as time goes by.

LCD units use liquid crystals, in units called pixels, to paint a picture of the bottom on the screen. The better models have many features, such as zoom, bottom lock, fish alarm (yes, they will actually find fish), bottom alarm (which tells you you are reaching a preset minimum depth level), and a memory feature that lets you store the picture of the bottom for future reference.

The better units are compact, relatively inexpensive when compared to the paper graph units, and waterproof so they can stay on the boat in all types of weather.

I find the electronics useful for finding probable fishing areas in water too deep to sight-survey. By using these units I can locate underwater rock formations, piles of sunken brush, or other fish-holding structures that would be impossible to find otherwise.

My real education came when I went to spots that had produced fish in the past, and was able to see why the fish had always held there at certain times of the year. Armed with this knowledge, it was possible to use the LCD to look for similar areas.

Many good river fishermen never use electronic sonar and such equipment isn't absolutely necessary. But I feel that, with one in use on your boat, you will become a better fisherman.

Trolling Motors

An electric trolling motor may seem like a luxury for a riverboat, but after you have one, you will probably consider it a necessity. A foot-controlled, bow-mounted trolling motor allows you to maneuver your boat without using your hands, and a good heavy-duty motor with plenty of thrust will allow you to hold in heavy current and thoroughly fish selected areas.

A trolling motor for river fishing should have at least thirty pounds of thrust for fishing in current, and most of us have found that the twenty-four-volt models work better for river fishing where you will be using the motor hard and often, fighting the current. Having to keep two batteries charged and ready is a problem, but the advantages of twenty-four-volt make it worth it in my mind.

SPECIAL PURPOSE BOATS

The principal problem facing the riverboater is shallow water. Over the years many different approaches have been tried to protect the propeller and lower unit of a regular outboard, such as fastening a pitchfork to the lower unit or building a rock guard. The following types of boats avoid this problem either by moving the propeller from its traditional position below the boat or by eliminating it entirely.

Airboats

A type of propulsion that has been tried in parts of the Susquehanna River is the airboat. This is the boat of Everglades fame that uses a

Airboats are popular on certain sections of the Susquehanna River.

large propeller mounted above the water's surface to drive the board by air. The boats do have merit. There is no lower unit hanging under the boat to hit submerged rocks, and the boats will go in water where outboards cannot run.

The downside of using the airboat is that the setup is expensive. The motor that turns the propeller is usually an air-cooled auto engine, often from a Volkswagen. Another big problem is that the engines are usually quite noisy to operate—so noisy, in fact, that I found the entire experience, after riding in two different rigs, quite unpleasant.

Jet Boats

An alternative to the airboat, with many of the same benefits, is the jet boat. In this configuration, the lower unit of a propeller-driven outboard is replaced with what is basically a pump. Water is sucked in through one port and expelled from another, creating the thrust to drive the boat.

Jet boats have been popular in Alaska and other areas for many years, but have only begun to catch on along the Potomac over the past few years.

The places a jet-driven boat can run are amazing. Once the boat has broken out into a plane, it can run literally in inches of water. A friend showed me this by running upstream through some very shallow flats with no difficulty, and then attempting to drift back. With the boat down from plane, we found that there absolutely just wasn't enough water to float the boat back downstream without constantly hitting bottom. As one boater explained it, "If it's wet, you can run there on plane."

There are, of course, problems. One is the price. At this time replacing the lower unit with a jet unit for a forty-horsepower outboard costs about $1,500. And then you are stuck with a perfectly good propeller type lower unit that you no longer have any use for.

Many of the river anglers go even one step further. They install a tunnel in the boat that helps supply the motor with water, allowing them to raise the pump to a level flush with the bottom of the boat. To make the tunnel, a section measuring approximately thirty inches long and ten inches wide is taken out from the transom forward. Then a tapered tunnel is welded into the hole. The tunnel then shunts water to the pump unit of the jet outboard.

Another cost consideration to be given to the jet boat is that the hull of the boat must be heavier than most boats because, even with the advantage of jet drive, encounters with rocks and ledges are going to occur. Most jet experts recommend a hull from .100-gauge aluminum, and a boat from this heavy stock costs more than the average aluminum boat.

Another disadvantage is that in going to the jet you will lose about 30 percent of the output. In other words, if you are running a fifty-horsepower outboard, and install a jet drive lower unit, you are dropping to about thirty-five horsepower in terms of output or top-end speed. Jet owners, however, all seem happy to trade the power for the shallow water capabilities.

Buying a full-rigged boat such as the Potomac River regulars are using is an expensive proposition. A fully rigged sixteen-foot heavy-aluminum boat, plus a fifty-horsepower engine with jet drive and an electronic trolling motor, is now costing $8,000–$12,000. But many must feel the advantages justify the price because the dealers say they are selling them as fast as they can get them in.

CANOES

Lefty Kreh once told me that if a river fisherman could only have one boat, it should be a canoe. I'm inclined to agree. Although my big boat gets the most use during my hours on the water, the canoe is invaluable for certain situations, such as fishing smaller rivers like the South Branch of the Potomac.

Canoes offer many advantages for river fishermen. They are shallow-draft boats that are easy to maneuver, and light enough to be carried into hard-to-reach put-in and take-out spots. Having a canoe will allow you to fish areas that many fishermen can't get to.

A canoe for fishing should be stable, first of all, and you should look for a wide, flat bottom, as opposed to the long, narrow boats designed for white water and speed.

Several materials are used in modern boats, including fiberglass, Kevlar, other space-age plastics, and aluminum. The synthetics offer the advantage of being quieter when the hull comes into contact with rocks or paddles, but the good aluminum boats are well built and, despite the dents that accumulate over the years, will last for a very long time. I doubt if you could wear one out.

The early river fishermen found the canoe a perfect vessel for river navigation and, over the years, we have done little to change the basic design of that the Indians used. The canoe remains the ideal design for a self-propelled river craft.

FOUR

Tackle

The manufacture and sale of fishing tackle is a highly innovative and highly competitive business. Each year, new and better equipment is introduced to the marketplace, and the advances in tackle are one of the reasons that the modern angler is so much more effective on the stream.

The rods and reels being produced at this time feature the latest in high-tech engineering and manufacturers' processes, and are constructed of modern materials such as graphite and boron. The result is equipment that is lighter, tougher, and more functional than ever before.

With all the new products on the market, it is sometimes hard for the relative beginner to make an intelligent choice when buying new tackle. In this chapter, we will look at the different types of tackle used when fishing the rivers of the mid-Atlantic and what types of tackle are used for the different species of gamefish.

MATCHING THE TACKLE TO THE FISH

When choosing the tackle you will buy on your next trip to the sporting goods store, the key point to remember is to match your tackle to the fish you want to catch. For example, if you are mostly a smallmouth fisherman, you will need different tackle than the person who trolls big plugs in the New River for muskies. If you think this sounds like you need a lot of different tackle to cover all the different fishing situations that are found on the rivers of the mid-Atlantic, you're right. The truly versatile fisherman owns many types of fishing tackle and knows how to use them all.

SPINNING TACKLE

Spinning tackle is probably the most popular type of tackle used on the rivers. You can purchase spinning tackle in a size to fit almost any fishing situation, and it is fairly easy for the beginner to learn to use.

The very mechanics of spinning tackle, with the line flowing freely from the spool when the bail is released, makes casting light lures on light line easy and, since many river fishing situations call for light-weight lures and light lines, spinning tackle is the logical choice to start with.

Over the past several years the tackle manufacturers have made many improvements in the spinning tackle offered for sale in local tackle shops, and the very nature of the tackle business is such that the items that are new today will probably be outdated within the next few years. However, we will look at some of the features on the modern spinning reel.

Spinning Reels

One of the biggest changes over the past few years is the extensive use of graphite in making reels and reel components. Graphite has several advantages over other materials, but the biggest advantage is its relative light weight and its resistance to corrosion or rusting.

Anther feature that most modern reels have is the highly adjustable drag located on the back of the reel where it can easily be changed—even while fighting a fish. However, it has been my experience that many of the stern drag systems currently in use leave much to be desired. A friend in the tackle industry explained that there is a power transfer problem in the design, and consequently many stern drags require a large initial surge to get the drag started slipping. In other words, a drag that slips smoothly at five pounds of pull may take up to eight or nine pounds of pull to get the drag started slipping.

Obviously, if your line has a breaking strength of eight pounds, and your drag requires a nine-pound surge to start slipping, you are going to lose a lot of big fish.

The folks in the tackle industry are aware of the problems in their products; by the time you read this, the drags on the top-quality spinning reels may be working perfectly. However, if possible, you should test the drag on the reel before you buy it. Many tackle shops will gladly let you do so before you lay your cash on the counter.

Another feature found on many of the better spinning reels is a lever on the bail that allows you to reach down with the index finger of your right hand, grasp the line, and trip the bail without using your left hand. The different companies have different names for this feature and the promotional people tell me that the public really likes this new feature. But I must have spent too many years using my left hand: even though many of my reels have this feature, I still use my left hand to trip the bail.

Spinning Rods

All rods are not created equal, and every rod is a compromise of some sort or another. Always keep this in mind when choosing a rod—spinning, bait-casting, or fly rod.

For example, not everyone realizes it, but a short rod is better than a long rod for fighting a big fish. And a short rod is nicer to cast. Many fishermen, particularly bass fishermen, who make hundreds of casts per day, have gone to the short rods.

On the other hand, the longer rod is more forgiving, particularly when you're using very light lines, so if you are interested in using lightweight lines for big fish, you would want a fairly long spinning rod with plenty of parabolic action to absorb the movements of the fish.

Most serious bass fishermen are now using rods made of graphite or boron, and have gone to shorter spinning rods, usually measuring between five and six feet in length. Such rods are light and powerful, which makes all-day casting pleasant, and the relatively stiff and sensitive graphite and boron spinning rods make strike detection easy.

The spinning rods that I like best are one-piece rods, with a cork or graphite handle that the rod passes through. The rod should have a fairly fast tip that allows the casting of lightweight lures, but should also have plenty of reserve strength in the butt for setting the hook and for fighting a nice fish.

BAIT-CASTING TACKLE

One of the most important developments in the fishing tackle world over the past few years has been the increased interest in bait-casting tackle. This interest has been sparked by recent improvements that make it possible for the average fishing nut to cast a fairly light lure or bait on casting tackle without experiencing the infamous bird's nests that were common with the old bait-casting, or revolving-spool, tackle.

There are certain fishing situations where bait-casting tackle excels. One that immediately comes to mind is fishing surface lures. The usual method of fishing a surface lure is to cast out, let the lure settle, and then pop or twitch the lure with the rod tip. You then gather up the slack line created by the rod movements, and manipulate the lure again.

Most fishermen using spinning tackle for surface-lure fishing sooner or later experience the result of picking up slack line on a spinning reel. On a subsequent cast, a big ball of line will come hurtling off the reel to hang up in the first rod guide.

I also like bait-casting tackle better for fishing live bait because you can put the reel out of gear and let the fish run with the bait while you thumb the reel to prevent overruns. I find it much harder to use spinning tackle for this purpose.

Before recent improvements—most notably magnetic controls—were incorporated into bait-casting reels, it was difficult for the average angler to cast light lures without experiencing the tangles that occur when the spool is turning faster than the line is going out. However, with the modern magnetically controlled bait-casting reels, backlashes are far less common and almost anyone can learn to cast effectively with a few minutes of practice.

The principle behind the magnetic controls currently being used by tackle manufacturers is a series of magnets on the left side of the reel that establish an adjustable magnetic field that slows the turning of the reel's spool and can be adjusted by a dial on the left side of the reel.

Most experienced casters use a low magnetic control setting and "thumb" the reel as the cast ends. However, the newcomer to bait casting can set the reel at one of the higher numbers and enjoy the benefit of a high degree of backlash control with only a small loss in casting distance.

The modern bait-casting reel is a precision instrument, and is priced accordingly. However, the reels are well made and will last for years if you follow the routine maintenance instructions that come with them.

Bait-Casting Rods

High-quality bait-casting rods are now being made of many materials, including fiberglass, graphite, boron, and composites of glass and graphite or glass and boron.

Many fisherman, after experiencing the increased performance that a graphite or boron rod delivers over the older fiberglass rods, now use graphite or boron exclusively. However, the better fiberglass rods are very fine fishing tools and should not be overlooked.

The most important thing is the action of the rod and, for most fishermen, a rod with a medium action—which means a fairly fast tip and plenty of butt strength—is preferred, although every person has his or her own ideas on how a rod should perform.

Over the past few years, with the tremendous growth of interest in bass fishing, the rods have been getting shorter and more powerful, and most of the bait-casting rods you will find on your dealer's shelves will be between five and six feet in length. However, longer rods do have applications in river fishing, particularly when you're fishing for the bigger fish like muskies, where a longer rod would be helpful in casting the big lures used for these fish.

Most of the bait-casting rods designed for freshwater fishing come with a pistol grip, which is comfortable and works quite well in most situations. But for heavier work, such as casting big baits for catfish or muskies, you might want to try a rod with a longer, straight grip (eight inches is usually a good length) that will allow you to grip the rod for two-handed casting. The light popping rods, which are popular in salt-water fishing, work well for this purpose.

SPIN-CASTING TACKLE

Although spin-casting tackle is often looked down upon by the so-called experts as the tackle of beginners or children, the popularity of this tackle continues to grow. Spin casting is a kind of compromise between spinning and bait-casting tackle, and is probably the easiest tackle for the beginner to learn to use.

It seems that every kid starts out with spinning-casting tackle (I know I did), but this doesn't necessarily mean that it's for kids only. Over the years I've met many bona fide expert anglers (people who catch more trophy fish in one season than the self-professed experts catch in five) who use spin-casting tackle exclusively and hardly seem hampered by their choice.

Although spin-casting tackle can be bought that will handle very light lines and, in turn, light lures, the tackle seems to perform best in the medium-light category. This would mean a line weight from eight- to twelve-pound test, with a rod to match this type of tackle.

Spin-Casting Reels

Spin-casting reels utilize the property of spinning reels in which the line comes off a stationary spool (versus coming off a revolving spool with bait-casting gear), but the spool is covered with a housing and the line passes through a hole in the center of the housing. The line is released by pressing a button on the back of the reel, and even small children can learn to cast in a few minutes. Another of the things that make these reels attractive to so many anglers is that they are usually priced lower than spinning or bait-casting models.

Spin-casting reels mount on standard bait-casting rods.

One final word on spin-casting tackle: If you are using it and doing well with it, don't let the "experts" pressure you into changing. There's an old saying that covers this situation: "If it ain't broke, why fix it?"

FLY-FISHING TACKLE

One of the biggest misconceptions in the fishing world is that fly-fishing is an elitist sport, practiced only by eccentrics who are more interested in showing off their expertise and expensive equipment than in catching fish.

Every season I run into anglers who tell me that fly-fishing sure looks like fun, but they feel that it would be too difficult to learn, and besides, they aren't artists and would never be able to tie those beautiful flies that are used. This is simply nonsense, and what's worse is the fact that many people involved in the sport of fly-fishing do their best to perpetuate these misconceptions.

The truth of the matter is that fly-fishing isn't any more difficult than other types of fishing; it's simply different. When you cast with spinning, bait-casting, or spin-casting tackle, you use the weight of the lure or bait to take the line out. In fly casting, you use the weight of the fly line to take the lure (fly) out.

Since this is a book on river fishing in general and not on fly-fishing, I will only go over choosing a basic fly-fishing outfit for river fishing. But if you are interested in learning more about the sport, there are many excellent books on the subject. Two that I recommend highly are *Fly Fishing: A Beginner's Guide* by David Lee, and *Fly Casting with Lefty Kreh* by Lefty Kreh.

Fly-fishing tackle is rated by the weight of the line the fly rod is designed to handle. Fly lines come in several tapers. (Taper is the variation in the diameter of the line from back to front; for example, a level fly line is the same diameter throughout its length, while a weight-forward fly line is thicker in the front, which concentrates the weight at that end for easier casting. Other tapers that are available include double taper, bug taper, and saltwater taper.)

The least expensive fly line is the level fly line, because it is easier (and thus cheaper) to manufacture; however, if you are buying a line for river fishing, I would recommend a weight-forward, floating line. It will cost a little more than a level line, but will be far easier to cast.

Fly lines are also rated by weight and classified according to standards developed by the American Fishing Tackle Manufacturers Association (AFTMA). The larger the numerical designation, the heavier the line. A light, 3-weight fly line would be used for trout fishing on small streams, while a big 12-weight line would most often be used for casting to large saltwater gamefish.

For most river fishing a 6-, 7-, or 8-weight outfit will be ideal. I personally use an 8-weight most of the time, but have friends who swear by a 6-weight outfit.

Fly Reels

The reel for river fly-fishing can be any single-action fly reel that will hold the fly line and thirty or forty feet of backing. There are many fine single-action fly reels on the market that will work quite well. Stay away from the automatic fly reels—they are heavy, the drags don't work, and they seldom have enough spool space for backing. One type of fly reel I do like is the multiplying reel, which has a gear ratio of three to one. In other words the spool turns three times for each turn of the reel handle. I find this handy for keeping the line up when fishing from a boat.

Fly Rods

The most expensive part of the fly-fishing system is the fly rod. You can buy fly rods that cost over $300 or you can buy a perfectly serviceable rod for less than $100. Most modern fly rods are made of graphite, or a composite of graphite and fiberglass, and a few are made of boron. In addition, a few good fiberglass rods are still being made, and usually cost less than graphite rods. The S-glass fiberglass rods are very fine casting fly rods.

The length of the fly rod is also important. With the increased use of graphite, which made fly rods lighter, many fly fishermen went to longer rods for river fishing—usually 8½- or 9-footers. A long rod has many advantages, such as increased line control and easier casting, but, for the beginner, an 8- or 8½-foot fiberglass or moderately priced graphite fly rod, rated for a 6-, 7-, or 8-weight line will work just fine. I really can't recommend a rod any less than eight feet in length for river fishing.

After you have secured a fly rod, reel, and fly line, you will need a leader. The leader attaches to the end of the fly line and is tapered. In river fishing, a long, complicated leader is seldom needed, and a store-bought leader, seven to nine feet long, that tapers to a six-pound-test tippet, will be fine for most situations.

Over the years, I've run into very few fishermen who use all types of tackle—spinning, bait casting, and fly rodding. This is a shame because, by limiting themselves to fishing with one type only, they are missing many opportunities that another type of tackle might make available. You can't really fish a caddis or mayfly hatch well with anything other than fly rod tackle, and when jigging for early season walleyes or smallmouths, nothing works better than light spinning gear.

The complete river fisherman should learn to use all types of tackle; with the many new instructional books and videos on the market, learning to use each type isn't nearly as hard as many fishermen seem to believe.

FIVE

Artificial Lures and Live Bait

ARTIFICIAL LURES

There are literally thousands of artificial lures on the market, designed to swim, dive, pop, gurgle, rattle—just about everything but burp.

Choosing the lures to carry in your tackle box is, at best, a confusing proposition. For the beginner the best bet is to try to find an experienced local fisherman who can put you on the right track as far as what lures are the most popular in your area.

There are a few old standards that have withstood the test of time and appear in almost every fisherman's tackle box; they should also be present in yours. In this chapter we will look at the different types of artificial lures that are used on the rivers, and I will point out some of the lures that have proven effective.

Floating/Diving Lures

The floating/diving lure, such as the Rapala or the Rebel Minnow, is one of the most versatile types of lures ever designed. This type can be used as a surface lure by casting it out and retrieving with twitches across the surface, or it can be cast out and cranked back, which will cause it to run just beneath the surface with an enticing wobble that most gamefish find irresistible.

Floating/diving lures come in all sizes, from tiny two-inch models that are great for panfish and smallmouth bass, to huge models designed primarily for saltwater use. The bigger models are very popular in the rivers that contain muskies.

Every river fisherman's tackle box should contain a selection of the floating/diving lures. The 3-inch and 4½-inch models are good lengths to invest in and the following color combinations have proven effective over the years: silver sides, black back; silver sides, blue back; and gold sides, black back.

32

Selection of crankbaits for river fishing.

Crankbaits

The generic term crankbait is somewhat undefined, as certain writers use the term to describe many types of lures, including the floating/diving lures. However, for our purposes, crankbaits are lures that are designed to be fished underwater exclusively, and that are fitted with lips that cause them to dive when retrieved. Crankbaits come in many sizes and configurations, and some swim just beneath the surface when retrieved, while others can reach depths of ten feet or more when retrieved.

Crankbaits are generally designed to imitate small fish; however, a few lures are shaped to imitate crayfish and are designed to crawl right on the bottom where fish would expect to find a crayfish. Crankbaits come in almost every imaginable color, and a selection of crankbaits in different sizes and weights should be part of your river fishing arsenal.

In the interest of simplicity, we can divide crankbaits into two categories: shallow-running crankbaits that fish just beneath the surface, and deep-diving crankbaits that will scrape the bottom in eight to ten feet of water.

Bottom bouncing lures: top row, *plastic worms on slider heads;* bottom row, *rubber-skirted jigs with pork rind and plastic worm trailers.*

In the shallow-running crankbait category, lures that have proven effective include the Big-O (¼-ounce model) by Cordell, the Little "N" by Norman Lures, and the Model A by Bomber Lure Company. Deep-diving lures that I have used with success include the Deep-Wee R by Rebel Lures, the Wiggle Wart and Wee Wart by Storm Lures, and the Deep Little "N" and Deep Baby "N" by Norman Lures.

The "best" colors would be hard to pin down, since there are so many available, and they tend to change from year to year. The brown and orange lures (usually called "crawfish" by the tackle companies) normally work well, as do lures with chartreuse coloring; and the silver- or "shad"-colored lures which seem to most closely imitate small baitfish are usually very popular.

Surface Lures

Many fishermen feel that catching fish on surface lures, also called topwater lures by bass fishermen, is one of the most thrilling methods of fishing the rivers of the mid-Atlantic. The splashing strike of a hungry smallmouth as it attacks a surface lure is certainly one of the most

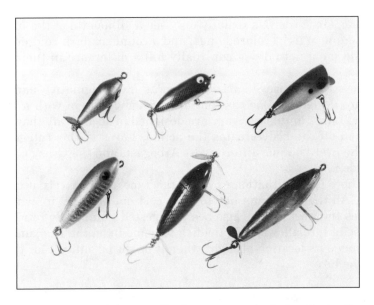

Top water lures. The propeller lures are particularly effective for river bass.

exciting sights in river fishing, and at times it seems that surface lures take more than their share of trophy fish.

There are many types or designs of surface lures that will work well on the rivers, but two types in particular—the lures with propellers on one or both ends, and the type I call steady-retrieve lures—seem the most popular.

The propeller lures (like the Tiny Torpedo and Baby Torpedo by Heddon; the Devil's Horse, Buck & Bawl, and Horsefly by Smithwick; and the Hellraiser by Whopper Stopper) are characterized by propellers that churn the water when the lures are twitched or retrieved. Most propeller lures are made of plastic, but certain companies like Smithwick still make their lures from wood, and I have to admit to a certain fondness for the wood over the plastic, although the fish-catching ability of one over the other may only be in my mind.

The usual method of fishing the propeller lures is to cast them out and then retrieve them by manipulating the rod tip, causing the lures to twitch and pop while the propellers churn the water. An irregular, popping retrieve is usually the best.

As for colors, I can't really say that I prefer one over the others. I've always thought that the color of a surface lure was pretty much academic, since the fish usually only see a silhouette of the lure. So buy a couple of light-colored ones, and a couple of dark-colored ones, and drop me a note if you can really tell a difference in their effectiveness.

The steady-retrieve surface lures, as my imaginative name implies, are designed to be cast out and brought back in with a steady retrieve. Lures in this category are designed in such a way that water deflection off the body creates the action. Lures in this category include the ever-popular Jitterbug by Arbogast, and the Crazy Crawler by Heddon.

If there is one situation in which this type of lure excels, it is night fishing. All the fisherman has to do is cast out and reel in, while the lure does the work. It has also been suggested that steady retrieval of this type of lure allows the gamefish to home in on the lure and accurately judge its location at night when it might be difficult for the fish to see the lure.

Spinners, Spinner Baits, and Buzz Baits

Spinners and spinner baits are two of the more versatile lures you can add to your tackle box. By varying the speed of the retrieve, you can fish the lures at any depth, from right on the surface to bumping along the bottom.

There are basically two type of spinners: the simple in-line type, as characterized by the Mepps and Roostertail brands, and the "safety pin" style of spinner, usually called a spinner bait.

Spinners and spinner baits are unusual lures in that they don't seem to imitate any particular forage specifically, but rather attract fish with a combination of flash and noise or vibrations from their churning blades.

The in-line spinners are noted fish catchers, taking everything from the little panfish to muskies, depending on the size of the spinner.

The spinner bait is best known as a bass lure although, in the smaller sizes used for smallmouths, it will sometimes take panfish, and the larger sizes have been known to fool the occasional muskie.

The buzz bait is simply a spinner bait with larger, cupped blades that chop the surface, helping to keep the lure on top of the water and creating a very large, "buzzing" disturbance.

Fishermen sometimes call buzz baits "aggravation" lures, thinking that the annoying commotion of a splashing buzz bait provokes reflex strikes.

Spinners and spinner baits: top, *inline spinner;* bottom left, *spinnerbait;* right, *buzz bait with plastic grub trailer.*

Jigs for river bass and panfish: top row, *plastic action-tail jigs;* bottom row, *marabou jigs.*

*Bucktail jigs and pork rind trailers are tops
for big smallmouths.*

Spinners, spinner baits, and buzz baits can be modified to suit the angler by having trailers added to the hook, usually in the form of a plastic worm, grub, or piece of pork rind. Many anglers also like to fasten a trailer or "stinger" hook to the lure, which helps hook short-striking fish that grab onto the trailer or skirt of the lure and usually escape getting hooked.

Flies
River anglers who use fly tackle have an opportunity unmatched by anglers using other tackle in that they can imitate virtually any type of food the fish are feeding on, from the smallest aquatic insects to the largest forage fish.

The listing of all the many flies that work well in river fishing situations is a subject far beyond the scope of this book, where we are looking at all types of tackle. As a basic guide, however, the types of flies needed would fall into one or another of the following categories.

Poppers and Popping Bugs

Poppers and popping bugs are designed to be fished on top of the water, and when they are retrieved, they create a surface disturbance or "pop" in the water.

There are many designs and types of poppers, but a good beginning selection should include something like the cork Potomac River Popper, which is nothing but a bottle cork with a flattened bottom and a short tail made from bucktail or squirrel tail.

Another popular popper type is called a pencil popper. The pencil popper is made from a small cylinder of plywood, tapered at the back and mounted on a long-shank hook. When bass are chasing minnows in shallow water, this popper can be deadly.

One of the oldest popper types is the deer hair popper. Hollow, buoyant, deer hair is spun onto the hook and trimmed to shape. This popper usually offers a more subtle surface action, and at times seems more to the liking of fish in shallow water. A variation of this is the muddler type fly, which is a streamer body with a spun deer hair head. This is one of my favorites, and will take smallmouths as well as any surface fly I have tried.

Selection of flies for river fishing: left to right, top row, *Potomac River Popper, Pencil Popper, Dahlburg Diver;* middle row, *All Hackle Streamer (red and white), Zonker;* bottom row, *Clouser Crayfish, Black Marabou Leech.*

Another variation of the deer hair popper is a relatively new fly called the Dahlburg Diver. This fly combines the deer hair body with a collar of hair that has been treated with a glue to make it stiff and waterproof. When the fly is retrieved with a short, quick pull, the fly's collar forces the fly to dive; when the pull stops, the fly rises back to the surface. This gives you much the same effect as a floating/diving spinning lure such as the Rapala.

Poppers will take many of the river fish, but are best for bass and panfish. Most fly rodders prefer taking fish on the surface when possible and seem to agree that it's the most exciting type of fly-fishing.

Streamers

Streamers are flies that imitate minnows; and, since the bigger fish that most of us prefer to catch eat minnows, streamers are a good choice for many situations.

There are several streamer patterns that work well, including the Zonker pattern, the Marabou Streamer, and various bucktail patterns. One of my favorites is a black sculpin that is made with a deer hair head and a wing of black rabbit fur like the Zonker. Rabbit fur and marabou are favorite streamer materials for smallmouth bass because of their lifelike movements as they undulate in the currents of the water.

Streamers can be fished just beneath the surface with an unweighted pattern, or right on the bottom with a weighted pattern or by weighting the leader with lead. Most streamers are designed to be worked near the surface or at mid-depth, but the sculpin patterns should be weighted and fished right on the bottom, which is where fish expect to find the sculpins and stonecats that the flies imitate.

Nymph and Crayfish Patterns

The nymphal stage of a great many aquatic insects is an important part of the diet of river fish, and almost every species will take properly presented nymph flies. Nymphs for river bass fishing need not be as exacting in the imitation of the real fly as is the case when fly-fishing for trout, but more suggestive in character. A few generally imitative patterns such as the Hare's Ear or similar fuzzy nymphs made of fur in different natural colors such as tan, grey, olive, and black will usually do the job on the relatively unselective river fish.

Crayfish make up a very important portion of the diet of river fish, and a realistic crayfish fly is one of the most effective patterns.

I've tried several crayfish fly patterns, but the very best I've used is a design of Bob Clouser of Middletown, Pennsylvania. The fly is called the Clouser Crayfish, and meets all the requirements of a top fly pattern: realistic enough to fool fish with regularity, and yet durable enough to catch many fish before it becomes unusable, a fault many fly patterns have in common.

While using the Clouser Crayfish I've caught smallmouth bass, largemouth bass, catfish, walleye, rock bass, and sunfish, which shows how important crayfish are as a food source.

Bob runs a fly shop in Middletown (Clouser's Fly Shop, 101 Ulrich Street, Middletown, Pennsylvania 17057, 717-944-6541) and his crayfish pattern as well as the flies mentioned in this chapter can be ordered from him.

As you gain more experience in fly-fishing the rivers, you will find that the flies I've mentioned will only cover the basic requirements; and, if you are like most of us, you will soon be ordering (or, better yet, tying) many other patterns to meet the different situations you might encounter on the water.

The choosing of tackle and artificial lures and flies is very much an individual process. Every angler seems to develop strong opinions on what works best for him or her in different situations. But by trying some of the ideas in this chapter, and by following the rule of matching the equipment you use to the fish you are after, you will find hundreds of artificial lures and flies that will make your river fishing productive.

LIVE BAIT

There seems to be a commonly held conviction in fishing circles that live bait fishing is somehow less challenging than fishing with artificial lures. This is total nonsense, for to fish live bait, and to fish it right, is every bit as difficult as fishing any type of artificial lure.

The good live bait fishermen know what bait to use in certain situations, and how to rig and fish the bait so that it will be presented in as natural a manner as possible.

The following are some of the more popular live baits for river gamefish, and methods for presenting them.

Minnows

The generic term minnow, as used in this situation, applies to any small fish used for bait. In each river there are many different species of shiners, chubs, small suckers, small carp, and other small fish that can be used successfully as bait for smallmouth bass, largemouth bass, channel cats, or walleyes.

There are a number of ways of fishing minnows, but the most important thing to keep in mind, and this applies to fishing all live bait, is to use the smallest amount of weight necessary to get the minnow to the bottom, and to use thin-wire hooks that will do a minimum amount of damage when you impale the bait.

Or, if you want to cover more water, you can attach a split shot or two, make an upstream cast, and let the bait wash downstream with the current. Another method is to use little or no weight and attach a bobber to the line, and let the current and the bobber carry the minnow through likely holding water.

Size is an important consideration when choosing minnows to be used as bait. If there is such a thing as an average size, it would probably be between three and five inches long. However, many big bass and catfish experts routinely use six-inch chubs as bait and catch big fish on them. The old saying, "Big bait, big fish," seems to apply; but be advised that when using big minnows, you probably won't catch as many fish as you might with smaller minnows.

The Madtom Catfish

The marginated madtom catfish, also called stonecat or stony cat by fishermen, is a small catfish that lives under rocks and in weed beds. Madtoms don't grow very large—a five-incher is a big one—and are usually yellowish brown in color.

You might be wondering why madtoms weren't included in the section on minnow fishing; the reason is simple: These little cats are such good bait that they deserve a section of their own. I think it is safe to say without any qualification that stonecats are the very best bait you can find for taking large smallmouths during the summer months.

Stonecats are an ideal baitfish. They are extremely tough, and are easy to keep alive in a minnow bucket or on a hook. It's not unusual to catch four or five smallmouths on a stony and have the cat survive to be cast out again.

Madtoms are a big bait, and they naturally head for the bottom when you cast them out, so you seldom need any additional weight on the line. You can fish holes by casting the bait out and letting it sit on the bottom, or you can make an upstream cast into moving water and let the bait wash naturally downstream. But keep in mind that the little cats will attempt to hide under rocks, so if you are anchored and fishing a hole, you should move the bait occasionally to make sure it isn't hiding under a rock.

*Matthew Anderson with a trophy smallmouth
taken on the stonecat hanging from its jaw.*

The one bad thing about madtoms is that they are often hard to
come by. The most effective method seems to be seining weedy riffle
areas at night, when the the little catfish are most active. They are,
however, worth the trouble if you're interested in catching big smallmouths during the summer months.

Crayfish
The crayfish (also called crawfish or crab) is, without question, one of
the most important foods for river gamefish, but is also one of the hardest live baits to fish successfully. This is because the fish are used to
finding the little critters crawling along the bottom, and it's hard to
hook a crayfish and have it behave naturally.

However, I've met a few fishermen who use crayfish successfully,
and their tactics follow the ideas expressed earlier on fishing with minnows. They use thin-wire hooks and as little weight as practical. *If* the

currents allow, it's often best to use no weight at all. But in even moderate current you will probably be forced to add a split shot or two to keep the bottom, and that's exactly where a crayfish belongs—right on the bottom.

Most fishermen prefer to hook the crayfish through the tail and to keep the crayfish from grabbing onto rocks or underwater debris, pull the claws off before using them as bait. It is also true that many fishermen swear by the effectiveness of soft-shelled crayfish. (Crayfish are, of course, crustaceans and, as they outgrow their shells, they shed their hard outer covering to grow a new one. During this molting stage, the crayfish is said to be a particularly succulent morsel for any gamefish lucky enough to find one.)

Hellgramites
The hellgramite is the larval stage of the dobsonfly, and is one of the very best baits for not only smallmouths, but also panfish, catfish, and almost every species found in the rivers.

Hellgramites spend three to five years in the river and reach lengths of up to four inches. The hellgramite is dark brown to black in color and its most distinguishing characteristic is the pair of pinchers found near its mouth. The critter is less formidable than it looks, although it can give you a pretty firm pinch with its pinchers.

Hellgramites are most effective when drifted through likely holding water with as little weight as practical attached to the line.

Most fishermen prefer to hook the hellgramite through the collar near the head, and one of the interesting aspects of the hellgramite is that they continue to catch fish after being killed and mutilated by previous strikes. Apparently fish find the smell of a hellgramite—alive or dead—a most powerful attractant.

Nightcrawlers
The lowly nightcrawler, though disdained by many bass fishermen, continues to be one of the most reliable live baits throughout the country.

Worms or nightcrawlers were probably the first bait most of us used, but when we graduated from simple tackle and worms fished beneath a bobber, we forgot that a properly presented nightcrawler will take fish when other baits might fail us.

The biggest mistake made when fishing nightcrawlers is wadding the worm onto the hook in a big blob. For maximum effectiveness, the 'crawler should be hooked only once through the body, which allows it to wiggle enticingly. The bump-and-grind of a fresh, lightly hooked nightcrawler has an almost hypnotic effect on fish.

If you still aren't convinced, remember this: The West Virginia state record smallmouth, a fish that weighed nine pounds, twelve ounces, was taken on a nightcrawler by a sixteen-year-old angler. Enough said?

CATCHING AND STORING LIVE BAIT

If you fish regularly with live bait, you will probably want to develop a system of catching your bait and storing it at home.

The following are some of the methods I've found successful for catching and keeping live bait.

Minnows

Most of the better bait species of minnows are found in small creeks. The best method of catching minnows is to seine the creeks with a commercial minnow seine. Many fishermen really enjoy this process, calling it almost as much fun as the fishing itself.

You can also use a dip style minnow net. This net is usually a four-foot-by-four-foot square and is baited with doughballs. The net is raised periodically to see if the minnows have found the bait.

Some anglers like to use a minnow trap to catch their bait, but my success with traps has been poor and most of the minnows I've caught in these traps have been on the small side.

Storing live minnows can be accomplished in a number of ways. Some fishermen use a perforated container that they place in a nearby stream. The inner tank of an old washing machine is often used. The water flowing through the holes keeps the bait alive. Unfortunately, there are people who will steal your bait, or even the entire container.

You can also store minnows in a basement tank. Livestock watering troughs make good minnows tanks, and Southern States sells a plastic model that is a good value. Aeration of the water can be accomplished with a big aquarium pump or by using a water pump to push the water from the tank through a section of perforated pipe. The streams of water from the holes in the pipe fall back into the tank, aerating the water.

Crayfish

I can usually get all the crayfish I want while seining for minnows. If you seine right on the bottom you will usually pick up crayfish along

Observant anglers will notice things like this dobsonfly egg on streamside rocks, which would tell them hellgramites are present (the hellgramite is the larval stage of the dobson-fly).

the way. You can also catch crayfish by carefully picking up stones in small creeks and watching for the crayfish as they scurry away.

Many anglers use traps very much like miniature lobster traps. The traps are baited with meat (usually chicken necks) and the crayfish apparently respond well to this method.

Crayfish should be stored like minnows in aerated water. They store well, but if they are overcrowded, they sometimes fight and can kill each other with their claws. You should also keep them well fed to prevent cannibalism.

Hellgramites

Hellgramites live in well-aerated waters such as riffles. The insects live under rocks and can be caught by carefully lifting flat rocks and looking for hellgramites clinging to the underside.

The preferred method of catching them takes two people. The first positions himself downstream of the rocks to be overturned, holding a seine into the current. The other turns over the rocks, watching for hellgramites. Hellgramites washed off the rocks by the current become entangled in the seine.

Hellgramites are relatively easy to keep alive. The best method is to store them with wet leaves or stream grasses in a cool place. Some anglers and bait shops prefer to keep them refrigerated, which makes the insects go dormant.

Nightcrawlers and Worms

Nightcrawlers are one of the easiest baits to procure. Just check out your lawn on rainy nights and you will probably find all the night-crawlers you can use. Worms can be dug from gardens or near mulch piles.

Nightcrawlers keep best in commercial worm bedding. Most tackle shops sell this bedding or you can make your own from a combination of mulch and dirt.

Your nightcrawlers should be stored in a cool place. In recent years, most bait shops have gone to refrigerated storage, which seems to work best.

Some anglers like the commercially raised red worms as a bait. They are readily available at most commercial bait shops, and walleyes and panfish seem to really go for the red worms.

Advanced live bait fishing is really an art. Many of the best river fish-ermen I've met are true specialists at this form of fishing and they catch more big fish of various species than do most of the artificial lure fishermen who scorn bait fishing.

Live bait is particularly effective when times are tough. When the fish are acting finicky toward your artificial lures, live bait may be the way to tip the scales in your favor.

SIX

Smallmouth Bass

The smallmouth bass is the most popular gamefish found in the rivers of this book and, for that matter, one of the most popular in the country. The smallmouth displays all the qualities that endear a fish to anglers—they are found in good numbers throughout the mid-Atlantic area; can be caught using a wide variety of methods, baits, and lures; and, once hooked, put up a terrific struggle against the angler.

Many experienced anglers feel that, inch for inch, the smallmouth is the most sporting of the freshwater gamefish.

BIOLOGICAL INFORMATION

A few anglers have trouble distinguishing the smallmouth bass from its close cousin, the largemouth; however, when viewed closely, they are quite different. The smallmouth generally will appear to be slimmer, often showing dark bars along the sides, with a bright red eye, and body coloration that varies from a pale green to a deep bronze. When taken from clear, cool waters, the smallmouth is usually brown— hence the nickname bronzeback—but colors can vary a great deal according to the season and the diet of the fish.

Probably the best way to tell a smallmouth from a largemouth is by noting the hinge of the jaw. If the jaw hinge extends back past the middle of the eye it's a largemouth; if not, it's a smallmouth. You can also tell by the dorsal fin. On the largemouth, the dorsal fin will nearly be divided into two sections—a spiny section toward the front, and a soft section to the rear. On the smallmouth this separation is not nearly as distinct. However, after very little experience in handling both species, it is relatively easy to tell them apart.

AVERAGE SIZES AND TROPHY FISH

Although the average size of the smallmouths taken in the rivers covered by this book varies a great deal according to the river, the time of the year, and the skill of the angler, it would probably be safe to say that the average size in the course of a season would range from around eight inches to about fourteen inches. Those unfamiliar with the smallmouth might scoff at this relatively small average size, but even a ten-inch smallmouth can put up a nice struggle when taken on light tackle.

Many fishermen consistently take smallmouths larger than the average size, and a few consistently take fish much larger than average.

Which brings us to defining the term "trophy smallmouth." Obviously, this is a fairly subjective judgment, because one man's trophy could be another man's average fish. But most fishermen feel that any smallmouth weighing more than three pounds is a very nice one, and a four-pound smallmouth is a trophy by almost any standard. This four-pound mark, by the way, is also used by most states for the awarding of citations.

After going over the citation records from Maryland, Pennsylvania, West Virginia, and Virginia, I was able to determine that each of the rivers in this book has the potential of producing smallmouths weighing four pounds or more, but three of the rivers—the Potomac, the James, and the New—have the best track records of producing big smallmouths.

Since I write for the Hagerstown, Maryland, newspaper, I hear about many of the big smallmouths taken from the Potomac; over the past several years, fish weighing five pounds or more have been taken with a fair degree of regularity, and there have been several fish weighing more than six pounds taken.

Records from the states of Virginia and West Virginia show that the New River in Virginia and West Virginia regularly produces five-pound-plus smallmouths, with the occasional six-pounder, and the same is true for the James River in Virginia.

However, the biggest river smallmouth ever taken from the rivers covered by this book was caught from the South Branch of the Potomac River. This incredible fish weighed nine pounds, twelve ounces, and was caught on June 23, 1971, near Springfield, West Virginia.

This huge smallmouth was landed by David Lindsay, who at the time was but sixteen years old. The fish was 24¼ inches long and had a girth of nineteen inches. Scale samples were taken and the fish was determined to be nine or ten years old.

It is said that all records are made to be broken, but I feel that Lindsay's smallmouth is one record that may never be broken. A river smallmouth this large is about as rare as a 600-pound man, or a 400-pound whitetailed buck with a 20-point rack. Lindsay's smallmouth must surely rank as one of the great freshwater catches of all time.

FISHING TACKLE

As we have noted, the average smallmouth taken from the rivers of this book will probably be between eight and fourteen inches in length and weigh a pound or less. To enjoy such fish, you should choose your tackle accordingly. You can catch smallmouths on heavy tackle and winch them to shore or into the boat, but you'll get even more with a light or ultralight spinning or bait-casting outfit, loaded with four-, six-, or eight-pound-test line.

For most of my smallmouth fishing I use a lightweight spinning rod, usually a graphite or boron model, and a light spinning reel loaded with six-pound-test line. The rod I like best is the one-piece model with a cork or graphite handle that the rod runs completely through. Such rods give the anglers very good "feel," which is a big advantage when the fish are striking lightly.

However, when fishing certain types of lures, I prefer to use a light bait-casting outfit. This is particularly true when fishing surface lures, where I work the lure by giving it a twitch, and then pick up slack line with the reel. Many times picking up slack line will cause problems with spinning tackle, usually in the form of tangles on the next cast, but bait-casting tackle works perfectly. I also like bait-casting tackle for fishing deep-diving crankbaits, which often tend to overpower small spinning reels.

SMALLMOUTH LURES AND FISHING TECHNIQUES:
A SEASONAL APPROACH

Spring
The fishing season on most of these rivers can start much earlier than many people realize. The key factor is water temperature, and when the water temperature reaches 40 degrees, you can begin catching river smallmouths.

Right about now, I can hear the snorts from readers who don't start fishing until late April or May, and know for a fact that you can't catch smallmouths in water that cold. But the facts show otherwise; and not only can you catch smallmouths in 40-degree water, but it also has been proven—at least to my satisfaction—that the average size of the fish taken will be much larger than the fish you will be catching during the dog days of July or August.

Early spring fishing for river smallmouths is a somewhat specialized sport, requiring a knowledge of smallmouth habits and knowing

*Randy Wagner fooled this chunky smallmouth
with a jig during the early spring.*

where to look for the fish at that time of the year. The key word is
eddies. Eddies are created by cutouts in the bank, bends in the river,
and natural or man-made objects that deflect the flow of the current
and provide the fish with an opposite flow area that protects them from
the brunt of the main current.

The springtime smallmouth in 40-degree water are recovering
from a long, lean winter and are ready to feed. However, the metab-
olism of the cold-blooded fish does not allow them to actively chase
down prey in water this cold, so they take up stations in selected shoreline eddies and allow the current to wash the food to them.

The proven lure for taking the springtime smallmouth is a jig of
some type. Most Potomac River fishermen prefer a bucktail jig with a
pork rind trailer, weighing between ⅛ and ¼ ounce, depending on the
river level and the current.

The usual method of fishing the jig is to make an upstream cast
toward the head of the eddy and to fish the lure slowly downstream

This smallmouth liked the looks of a rubber-skirted jig topped with pork rind.

with frequent contact with the bottom. As the lure drifts downstream toward the boat, the angler should maintain constant contact with the lure and be ready to act instantly. Most strikes will be very subtle and if you aren't constantly on guard you will miss many of them.

Another jig material that has proven very effective in the springtime is marabou. Marabou jigs seem alive in the water and drop faster than jigs made of the buoyant bucktail; at times, the faster-sinking jigs seem to work much better. Although marabou does have a lot of built-in action, most fishermen like to add a trailer to the jig, but instead of the pork rind trailers most often used with a bucktail, the marabou jig is most often trailed with a small plastic grub or the end of a small plastic worm.

As spring advances and the waters warm, the bass will move into prespawning locations along the shorelines, and this period, usually running from late April through the month of May and sometimes into early June, is a great time to be on the water. The action is often fast and furious, although the average size of the fish taken is smaller than during the early spring period; the action is also more constant, and less skill is usually required to make an acceptable presentation.

Favored habit includes rocky shorelines, rocky points, and the gravel bars that the fish will eventually use as spawning beds. Most of the time the fish are to be found in relatively shallow water, ranging from two to four feet in depth, and they are usually aggressive when going after a lure or bait.

Top lures for the prespawn and spawning periods include the plastic grubs fished on light ($\frac{1}{16}$- or $\frac{1}{8}$-ounce heads) and small, shallow-running crankbaits. Floating/diving lures like the Rebel or Norman also work very well, particularly when the male bass are guarding the nest—a small floater/diver twitched slowly over a spawning bed is almost sure to draw a slashing strike.

Summer

The summertime is when the most fishermen are out and, generally speaking, is a productive time to fish. The rivers are usually at or near their shallowest flow of the year, and for many people this means donning an old pair of tennis shoes and faded jeans, and wading the rivers to escape the summer heat.

Most of the better summertime fishing occurs very early or very late in the day, before or after the midday heat. Just after dawn is one of my favorite times to be on the river. The air will be damp and cool and, if you are lucky, you will see the bass chasing minnows—making their last feeding runs before heading out to midriver to spend the day behind a ledge or rock.

Early and late in the day, you will often do well with surface lures, particularly those that feature propellers at one or both ends. Taking a nice river smallmouth on a surface lure is one of the most thrilling moments in river fishing. The lure makes a quiet plop down near the partially submerged log. You wait a second to let the ripples slowly spread away, and SPLASH! all hell breaks loose as a feisty smallmouth jumps all over the lure.

The Trophy Summertime Smallmouth

As we noted earlier, summertime is when the most fishermen are out, but for most anglers it is also the hardest time of the year to take big bass on a consistent basis. When you think about it for a moment, though, it makes sense.

Summer is a time of plenty in the rivers. The food supply is at its highest, and the rivers are at a low flow rate. This means the bass can live almost anywhere they want to and, when they feel like feeding, they can be picky about what they want to eat.

Now, for the angler, this creates a bad situation. In the springtime and late fall, when many of us catch most of our bigger fish, the rivers are up, and the fish are forced into certain types of eddies to escape the currents. In the early spring and late fall the food supply is also down, and the fish that want to feed cannot afford to be quite as choosy.

So the summertime angler, interested in catching trophy smallmouths, has the odds against him or her. The big fish aren't concentrated like they are during the spring and fall, and, with a riverful of food to eat, why should the bass take a chance on the plastic creation that doesn't look, smell, or act like the food that is so readily available?

There is a way, however, of getting the odds more in your favor in the summertime, and that's by using live bait. As the old song goes, "There ain't nothin' like the real thing, baby," and to the trophy river smallmouth, a fish that has lived in the river for eight or more years, nothing looks, tastes, feels, or smells more like the food it is used to feeding on than a live, wriggling specimen.

The following are some of the more popular live baits for river smallmouths, and methods for fishing them.

Smallmouth Live Baits—In most of the rivers of this book the smallmouth bass would be considered the number one predator. As such the bass have a wide variety of forage to choose from. All small fish are fair game (including young smallmouths) as well as crayfish and aquatic insects. In fact, bass have been known to eat almost anything. A friend caught a two-pound smallmouth several years back that had a young red-winged blackbird stuck in its throat.

Some baits are better than others, however, and during the summer months, using the right bait may mean all the difference.

The first thing to start with is minnows—creek chubs, river chubs, shiners, and various dace minnows. Most can be caught readily from smaller streams.

Hellgramites are a very good bait, but fishermen after trophy smallmouths often find themselves busy unhooking small fish and other less desirable species when using hellgramites.

On some rivers, crayfish are considered the top bait. On the Susquehanna River, anglers seem to fish more live crayfish than on any other river I've visited, but the crayfish is a primary forage on nearly every smallmouth river and stream.

For my money, the best bait for big smallmouths during the summer months is the madtom catfish or stonecat. If you have never used this bait you may doubt this claim, but once you try them you'll be a believer.

On the Potomac, the regulars have developed a method of fishing madtoms they call "floating a stonecat." When fishing madtoms via this method, they attach a bobber to the line according to the water depth, but seldom more than four feet above the bait. The fishermen then cast the bait out and let the boat and bait drift downstream with the current.

This is an extremely effective way of presenting the bait to the fish. The madtom is constantly fighting against the bobber as it drifts along, and you are covering large sections of the river, which increases your chances of coming into contact with a fish that is ready to feed. And, best of all, few trophy smallmouths can resist the temptation of nailing a big madtom when it goes wriggling by.

You can also fish minnows, hellgramites, or crayfish by floating them under a bobber, or you can use minimal weight and let the bait wash naturally along the bottom with the current.

The key to presenting any live bait is to make it appear as natural as possible. This means light lines, as little weight as possible, and thin-wire hooks that do minimal tissue damage to the bait.

When to set the hook after a bass takes the bait is a somewhat controversial matter. Many old-timers like to let the fish make its first long run, wait while the fish stops, and set the hook on the second long run. Others say that if the line is moving away, the fish obviously has the bait in its mouth and you can set the hook.

I've tried both ways, and now set the hook on the first run. In all honesty, I can't tell any difference in terms of the percentage of fish hooked. However, I think that by setting the hook on the first run you kill fewer small fish, and this is a most important consideration.

When fishing minnows, hellgramites, or nightcrawlers, you will hook many six- to ten-inch bass, and if you let them run they will swallow that bait and you will end up having hooked many of them in the gullet. Now the thing the experts say to do is to cut the line and leave the hook—that the fish will survive. However, I've always believed that many of them die. Can you imagine going about your business with a fishhook stuck in your belly? For this reason, I advocate setting the hook as soon as possible. By doing so, you will hook most of the little guys in the jaw where the fish can be easily released to fight another day.

FLY-FISHING FOR RIVER SMALLMOUTHS

I must admit to a distinct fondness for catching river smallmouths on fly-fishing tackle. It's not because fly-fishing is more sporting, or more effective. It's because catching river smallmouths on fly tackle is fun—nothing more, nothing less.

One of the most unfortunate things about this type of fishing is that many consider it an elitist (or, even worse, an incredibly complex) form of fishing that takes years to master. This is simply untrue. Learning to use fly-fishing tackle is no harder than learning to use spinning tackle well, or learning to use bait-casting tackle.

One of the best things about fly-fishing is that the river small-mouth fisherman can use an imitation of almost anything the bass likes to eat. Flies can be tied or bought to imitate the many insects, baitfish, or crayfish that the bass feed on, on a seasonal basis. No other form of fishing offers the angler such versatility.

Fly-Fishing Tackle

The most important pieces of fly-fishing gear are the rod and the line. It's an old saying, but still true, that in most freshwater situations, the fly reel is simply a place to store the fly line. I've caught many nice river smallmouths over the past few years, and seldom have I had to fight a fish off the fly reel.

Rods that work well for river smallmouths are from 8½ to 9 feet in length and rated for a 6-, 7-, or 8-weight fly line. As discussed in chapter 4, there are a number of materials currently being used for fly rods, and the angler can choose a model to suit his or her needs and budget constraints.

For an all-round rig to be used for river smallmouth fishing, I like an 8-weight outfit. Many of my friends use 6- or 7-weights and get by just fine. However, the smaller rods aren't as good for handling the bigger popping bugs that are used for river bass.

Your fly line can be a level or weight-forward taper. The level line is cheaper, but if you are serious about getting into fly-fishing, I would recommend buying the weight-forward line.

Any decent single-action fly reel will serve quite well for river smallmouth fishing, but you should have at least thirty feet of backing attached to the fly reel as insurance against that rare occasion when a big smallmouth (or catfish or muskie) hits at the end of a long cast and takes you into the backing.

To complete your fly-fishing outfit you will need some leaders 7½ to 9 feet long tapered to a six- or eight-pound-test tippet.

Flies for River Smallmouths

One of the problems with writing about flies for bass fishing is that bass flies aren't as standardized as trout flies. There are only a few nationally recognized patterns, and in each part of the country local tyers have adapted patterns to suit individual streams. Thus there are only a few basic designs, and that is the avenue we will take in talking about flies for river smallmouths.

Streamers

Over the past few years, rabbit fur streamers like the Zonker and the sculpin have become my favorite type. Rabbit fur is like marabou in the water, with quivering, undulating motions, but it is far more durable than marabou. For fishing just beneath the surface, a lightly weighted Zonker is hard to beat. My favorite colors are a brown body and black wing, and a silver body and white wing.

The sculpin pattern is a very good imitation of the madtom catfish, and a great fly for larger-than-average smallmouths. In the sculpins I like a brown body, black wing, and black deer hair head, and a brown body, brown wing, and brown deer hair head. Sculpins should be weighted to fish right on the bottom where the madtoms live, and where the bass expect to find them.

Nice river smallmouth and a selection of streamers and poppers.

Popping Bugs

For most of us, the fun way of taking river smallmouths is on popping bugs. And not only is it fun—many experienced anglers will tell you that popping bugs also take bigger bass than any other type of fly. Lefty Kreh tells of one September when he caught twenty-nine smallmouths weighing more than three pounds each on fly-fishing tackle. All of these trophy bass were taken on popping bugs.

Lefty, who has taken more trophy river bass than most of us will ever see, told me recently that he has never taken a smallmouth weighing more than four pounds on a streamer, but has taken dozens of trophy fish on popping bugs. The moral of all this is clear: If you are after trophy smallmouths on fly-fishing tackle your best chance is probably with a popping bug.

Popping bugs come in many sizes and shapes, and unfortunately many aren't worth bringing home. Those lavish, rubber-legged creations you see at many discount stores are usually poorly constructed and will not stand up to hard fishing. The best place to buy your poppers is from fly shops or mail order houses catering to fly fishermen that feature well-made bugs that will stay together.

The best bug I've tried is called the Potomac River Popper. This one was designed by Lefty Kreh, Irv Swope, and their friends from the Frederick, Maryland, area in the 1950s. The Potomac River Popper is simply a bottle cork cut flat on the bottom. The hook is mounted flush with the bottom of the cork, and a short, sparse bucktail or squirrel tail is tied on. The tail is kept short to prevent fouling while casting.

This bug is effective for several reasons. First, it is streamlined, lacking the heavy hackles and rubber legs found on many bugs. This makes it far easier to cast than other bugs of the same hook size. And second, mounting the hook flush with the bottom insures that the popper pops when twitched—and this bug pops better than any bug I've tried.

Deer hair bugs are also good, but aren't nearly as durable as bugs made of cork or balsa wood. Hair bugs are light and a pleasure to cast, and many tyers really enjoy making colorful deer hair bugs.

There have been many discussions about what color a bug should be, but in my opinion it's pretty much academic, because when a bass looks up at a popping bug all it sees is a silhouette or outline of the bug and gets a general idea of its size and shape. For that reason, all you really need are some light-colored bugs and some dark-colored ones. My favorite colors are white, yellow, and black. Use the yellow and white in bright light conditions and the black when it's cloudy or near dawn or dusk.

Nymphs and Crayfish Patterns

River smallmouths feed on immature aquatic insects more than the average angler realizes. Most river fishermen are familiar with hellgramites, but do not know about the many mayfly, stone fly, and caddis fly nymphs and larvae living in the river.

Fishing nymphs for smallmouths isn't as refined as nymph fishing for trout, where the fishermen use highly imitative flies. The nymphs used for bass can be more suggestive in nature and any large buggy-looking nymph will usually do the job. Western trout patterns like the Bitch Creek Nymph work very well for river smallmouths. The nymphs should be fairly large, and sizes 8, 10, or 12 will work well.

Crayfish are a prime river smallmouth forage, and flies that imitate the crayfish work very well. The most important aspect of a crayfish fly is that it be on the bottom, and for that reason most successful crayfish patterns are weighted rather heavily. As I mentioned earlier, the Clouser Crayfish is one of the best crayfish patterns I've tried to date.

Dry Flies

There are many insect hatches on the rivers this book discusses, and on most summer evenings you can enjoy fast and furious action by fishing large dry flies for the bass that are taking advantage of this food source. On average, the fish won't be large, but it's fast and fun fishing, and this is one time I like to use a light 4-, 5-, or 6-weight outfit, to enjoy the fight of the smaller bass.

As in choosing nymphs, the river smallmouth fishermen should pick a suggestive pattern rather than a highly imitative pattern, and I particularly like the big, hair-winged dry flies most often used out West for trout fishing. Patterns that work well include the Wulff patterns in white, brown, and grizzly in sizes 8, 10, or 12.

Fly-fishing Techniques

Since this is a general fishing book and not a fly-fishing book, we will look at these techniques in a quick general way. The easiest means to do so might be to describe how a typical day of fly-fishing might go on one of our rivers.

We start early, just after the sun is up, and as we drift slowly downstream, we have a Potomac River Popper knotted to our leader, and are casting toward the shoreline, which features downed trees and large rocks protruding from the water.

As the bug sits down, I like to give it one pop, and let it sit briefly before retrieving it with a steady popping retrieve. (River smallmouths seem to prefer a moving bug, as opposed to largemouths' taking the bug when it is stopped.)

As morning advances and the bass retreat from the shallow shorelines, we switch from the popping bug and begin casting a white Zonker streamer to partially submerged weed beds and underwater rock ledges. The Zonker is lightly weighted to fish just beneath the surface, and we retrieve it with short, erratic whips of the fly line to give the streamer a darting motion.

By midday, the action has slowed, so we anchor the boat near a large riffle, and wade into the pool below the riffle. This time we will use a big black nymph to imitate a hellgramite, or a crayfish pattern. The fly is cast upstream, and allowed to drift downstream naturally with the current. Smallmouths living in this type of water are almost always ready to feed.

The key to fishing the nymph or crayfish is to cast upstream and watch the fly line intently as it drifts down. You should retrieve the line to keep all slack out; when the line stops or twitches, set the hook. Sometimes it will only be a rock the fly has bumped into, but many times it will be a fish that has intercepted your fly.

In late afternoon, we notice a few white mayflies on the water, and see fish rising to take the duns and nymphs. Now is the time to tie on a large dry fly and cast to rising fish. This is a fine way to top off a day of fishing, and it's not unusual to hook and land thirty or forty fish in two hours during a good hatch.

Of course, we could also go back to the popping bug during the evening hours, which would be just as effective and would increase our chances of hooking a trophy fish.

Fly-fishing for river smallmouths is a fascinating sport, and one to which I could devote an entire book. In this chapter, we have covered live bait fishing, fishing with artificial lures using spinning and baitcasting tackle, and fly-fishing. Each method is effective under certain conditions, and to fully enjoy fishing for the river smallmouth—one of the great freshwater gamefish—I would encourage you to try each method.

SEVEN

Largemouth Bass

According to certain studies, the largemouth bass is the most popular freshwater gamefish in the country. This isn't surprising, given the largemouth's ability to live in a wide variety of water conditions, ranging from murky Florida swamps to silty farm ponds, and from tidal waters along the Atlantic Coast to the clear fresh waters of the rivers of the mid-Atlantic.

In the sections of the rivers we are looking at, the water conditions are better suited to smallmouth bass, but largemouths do live in each river, and in certain sections are found in good numbers. I've enjoyed excellent largemouth fishing in the slow-moving waters behind the dams on the Potomac, and on the Shenandoah River near Berryville, Virginia.

BIOLOGICAL INFORMATION

As we discussed in chapter 5, the largemouth isn't hard to tell from its cousin the smallmouth. Largemouths tend to be green in color and usually display a dark lateral line on each side, running the length of the fish. Also look at the jaw hinge—it extends past the middle of the eye.

AVERAGE SIZES AND TROPHY FISH

Largemouths grow larger than smallmouths, so the fish you catch will tend to be a little longer and heavier than a smallmouth from the same waters. On the Potomac where I do most of my fishing, the largemouths generally run from eleven to fourteen inches in length, and this seems to hold for largemouths I've taken from the other rivers.

The rivers do produce trophy largemouths, and in the sections of the rivers we are looking at, a four-pound largemouth is a very nice fish, so a five-pounder would be a real trophy. Larger bass are taken

61

each year, and a seven-pound largemouth is not out of the question in the better largemouth habitat sections.

TACKLE FOR RIVER LARGEMOUTHS

The light spinning and bait-casting tackle recommended for smallmouth bass will work just fine in most largemouth situations; since largemouths are often a bonus fish for anglers after smallmouths, they are most often taken on lightweight tackle.

However, you can use slightly heavier tackle when largemouth fishing, as the bass will take the bigger and heavier lures that may be too large for your lightweight spinning outfit. If I were choosing tackle strictly for largemouth fishing it would be a light spinning or bait-casting outfit that would handle ten-pound-test line well. The outfit should be capable of handling lures weighing from ⅛ to ½ ounce.

LURES AND TECHNIQUES FOR RIVER LARGEMOUTHS

The biggest difference in fishing for largemouths as opposed to fishing for smallmouths is that largemouths show a definite preference for holding near some type of shoreline structure like a downed tree, whereas the smallmouth is right at home in the middle of the river near underwater rock formations.

Other places that attract largemouths include weed beds, floating boat docks, sunken boats, or any type of natural or man-made cover that the fish can hide beside or behind.

On rare occasions, I've seen largemouths roaming about the river chasing baitfish, but more often the fish seem to prefer to take up ambush sites near cover of some sort, and let the baitfish come to them.

Artificial Lures

Largemouths will take a wide variety of lures, but one of my favorite methods of taking them is on surface lures. For fishing surface lures I usually like a light bait-casting rig and lures with propellers at one or both ends like the Smithwick Devil's Horse, or the Hellraiser by Whopper Stopper. Cast the lure to likely shoreline cover and retrieve with short pulls that cause the propellers to churn up the water. The difference between fishing surface lures for largemouths and for smallmouths is that largemouths generally seem to prefer striking a motionless surface lure, so you should make frequent pauses in your retrieve.

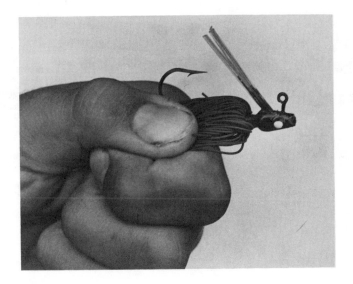

The plastic weed guard on this jig helps the angler fish heavy cover without snagging.

Another lure that ranks as one of the best for largemouths is a spinner bait. The design of a spinner bait makes it ideal for fishing the top of a downed tree, as the lure will bump its way through most obstacles without hanging up. I like to make the cast parallel to the trunk of a downed tree and retrieve it as close to the wood as possible.

Plastic worms are also proven largemouth lures; for river fishing, I like the four-inch worms fished on slider heads. The sliders are almost weedless and can be fished through the heavy brush and weeds that the largemouth really like. Slider heads are available in many weights, but for most river situations, ⅛- or ¼-ounce heads are heavy enough.

When the water temperature is below 60 degrees, jigs are probably the best lure to use. For largemouth fishing, the most popular jigs feature a living rubber skirt trailed with a pork rind frog. The jigs should have a weed guard of some type, and the favorite colors are black, brown, or a combination of black and brown.

Cast the jig and pork rind, or jig-n-pig, as they are called, to likely holding areas and, with the rod tip, slowly crawl the lure across the bottom while keeping all slack out by retrieving the line with the reel. Using this lure well takes some practice, but it is probably the best big bass lure you can use.

Largemouths like bigger jigs and pork rind, and the rubber-strand skirt topped with pork frogs is a favorite lure.

The other popular largemouth lure is a crankbait of some type. The size and diving characteristics of the lure should be dictated by the water depth you are fishing. Some of the best largemouth fishing I've had was behind a dam on the Potomac. The water was about sixteen feet deep, but the area was filled with sunken brush that came to within ten feet of the surface. The bass were holding in the top of the submerged brush; by using a crankbait that just barely reached the top of the brush, a partner and I took several big largemouths and didn't lose one lure to the brush.

This is a good example of using the right lure for the job at hand. When we tried a jig-n-pig on the brush pile, we were constantly getting hung. If we had used shallow-running crankbaits, we would not have reached the fish, which were ten feet down. But by using the right type of lure for the situation we were able to work the water that was holding the fish.

Live Bait for River Largemouths

It's been my experience that the largemouths living in the sections covered here aren't as interested in aquatic insects or crayfish as the river smallmouths are.

Rick Bingaman fooled this chubby largemouth with a small crank bait.

The few river largemouth specialists I've met use only one bait, and that's a large minnow—either a chub or a shiner—and fish the bait in certain spots known to hold largemouths.

The preferred method of fishing the minnow is to hook it through the lips, cast it out near holding areas such as underwater brush or floating boat docks, and let the minnow swim freely into the cover. If a largemouth is near, you are almost sure of attracting his attention with a big minnow.

Fly Rodding for River Largemouths

The same tackle and techniques outlined in the previous smallmouth chapter also work well for largemouths, with the only differences being that the largemouths will usually be found near shoreline cover, and they seem more interested in minnows than anything else. For that reason, I've never used nymphs or crayfish patterns for largemouths, although I'm sure largemouths eat these creatures on occasion.

Most of the largemouths I've taken on fly tackle have hit popping bugs. If you want, you can use bigger bugs than are commonly used for smallmouths, but it really isn't necessary.

Streamers worked near cover also produce well, and my best river largemouth struck a white Zonker streamer. The fish lived near a weed bed on the Potomac and hit the streamer like he hadn't had anything to eat for a month or more.

The largemouth isn't the number one gamefish in the waters we are looking at. The habitat isn't right for supporting large numbers of largemouths, and other species like the smallmouth and the channel catfish do much better in the rocky, flowing waters that are typical of these waters.

But largemouths do show up in certain areas, and wherever they are found they are always a favorite with anglers.

EIGHT

Walleyes

Walleyes are found in several of the rivers covered in this book, and when they are present in a river they attract a lot of attention from anglers. Walleyes grow to large sizes, will strike a variety of artificial lures and live baits, and are considered one of the the best tasting of the freshwater fishes.

As of this writing, walleyes are found in the Susquehanna, Juniata, Potomac, Greenbrier, and New rivers. Virginia is the one state that hasn't been actively stocking walleyes in their rivers. The Virginia biologists say that they prefer to concentrate on muskie stockings and feel that stocking both muskies and walleyes may cause the rivers to have too many predators.

However, Pennsylvania officials stock both walleyes and muskies in the Juniata and Susquehanna rivers, and say they haven't been able to document any problems from having both predators in the rivers.

BIOLOGICAL INFORMATION

Walleyes spawn in the early spring, when the water temperature reaches 40 to 48 degrees, and most spawning activity takes place at night. The eggs are usually deposited in a current (since walleye eggs need moving water to survive) and usually end up scattered randomly in rocks or gravel bottom in flowing water.

It should also be noted that walleyes are members of the perch family, very closely related to the yellow perch. Many people still call them walleyed pike, or river pike—including some well-published outdoors writers who should know better.

AVERAGE SIZES AND TROPHY FISH

One of the things anglers find most attractive about walleyes is that they grow to large size. In the Susquehanna and Juniata rivers in

Pennsylvania, walleyes weighing eight pounds or more are not uncommon. One of the biggest walleyes my research turned up weighed fourteen pounds, six ounces, and was caught in February 1984 from the Greenbrier River by Elmer M. Reed of Alderson, West Virginia. This is a very big walleye in any water.

In the Potomac, the walleyes were first stocked in 1979, so only a few fish have been around long enough to reach trophy sizes. However, at this writing, walleyes weighing up to five pounds have been taken.

It seems that if there is such a thing as an average size for the rivers we are looking at, it would probably be from fifteen to twenty inches in length.

TACKLE FOR RIVER WALLEYES

Although river walleyes grow to be big fish, the tackle used for catching them need not be heavy. Walleyes have a lot going for them as a gamefish, but flashy fighting technique isn't one of their characteristics—when hooked, the walleye tends to put up a dogged but unspectacular fight, staying deep and making a few determined runs before giving up. After you have hooked a few walleyes you can tell a walleye strike from the more-robust smallmouth almost immediately.

For most of my walleye fishing, I prefer a lightweight spinning outfit that can effectively handle six- to eight-pound-test line and light lures. The vast majority of the walleyes I catch each year are taken on light jigs, and a lightweight spinning outfit is best suited for fishing the small jigs.

LURES AND TECHNIQUES FOR RIVER WALLEYES

As we noted earlier, walleyes spawn in the early spring, and need moving water for spawning. This tends to concentrate the fish in certain areas, and one area certain to attract them during the spring spawning season is the riffle water below dams on walleye rivers. Top areas for spring walleyes are below Dam #4 on the Potomac River near Hagerstown, Maryland, and below the dams on the Susquehanna River near Harrisburg, Pennsylvania.

Other areas that attract walleyes in the springtime include pools below large natural riffles, or runs below man-made diversions such as wing dams, or even runs below big brush piles deposited by spring floods.

Artificial Lures

In the springtime, one of the best lures for taking walleyes is a jig of some type. You can use a bucktail jig, a marabou jig, or a plastic grub fished on a jig head. In my opinion, the weight of the jig is far more important than the material the jig is made of. Walleyes will always be near the bottom, and your jig should be heavy enough to make frequent contact with the bottom without constantly getting hung.

When looking for spring walleyes, you should concentrate your efforts in areas near moving waters. However, please note that the fish will be *near, but not in,* the heavy currents. Let me explain.

Walleyes are one of the most effective predators in the rivers. They like to be near moving water that will wash food to them, but they don't want to expend all their energy fighting heavy currents. For this reason they will hold on the *edge* of an eddy, where the swift water meets the eddy water. This is the number one feeding station—the fish can hold in the eddy currents, but still take advantage of any feed being washed by.

If you look at almost any section of river, you can find many such eddy areas. The eddy can be created by a very visible structure, such as a big rock bar that deflects the current, or it may be underwater and out of sight; but the eddy is there nonetheless.

To fish the eddies, you should position your boat slightly downstream of the potential fish-holding area, make an upstream cast into the current, and let your jig wash into the feeding station. In the swift waters walleyes are often found in, you will need a powerful trolling motor to hold the boat, or you can anchor within casting distance of the holding water.

Fishing a jig in such conditions and developing the sense of feel necessary to detect the usually subtle walleye strikes will take some practice, and you should be prepared to lose some jigs to the rocky river bottoms. But this is certainly one of the most effective methods of taking spring walleyes.

After the spring spawning season is over, the walleyes tend to disperse over large sections of the river and it becomes harder to find concentrations of the fish. However, areas that usually hold the fish on the Potomac are large underwater ledges—particularly those ledges that run across the river and have fairly deep water (at least three or four feet) behind them.

When the water temperature reaches 50 degrees, one of the best lures is a small crankbait, and you should choose your crankbait according to the water depth. Keep in mind that the fish will always be

Walleyes like small crank baits at certain times of the year.

near the bottom, so your crankbait should be making frequent contact with the bottom. Crayfish-colored crankbaits have proven particularly effective.

Jigs are also very good at this time, and motor oil– or smoke-colored grubs on a ⅛-ounce head have worked very well for me.

Live Bait for River Walleyes

Walleyes take a number of live baits well, but the two that have worked best for me have been nightcrawlers and small minnows. Nightcrawlers are popular with walleye fishermen throughout the country, and the river fish take them quite well.

There are a number of ways to rig the nightcrawlers, but the simplest way I've found is to use a thin-wire #6 hook, impale the crawler once through the middle of the body, and, with no weight (or a split shot or two added, depending on the current), cast upstream of likely holding water and let the crawler wash naturally with the current. This is particularly effective during the summer months when the fish become harder to coax into striking.

The same can be said for minnow fishing. The minnow should be hooked through the lips and drifted with the current. The one important factor in walleye fishing is that walleyes show a distinct preference for small minnows, and will take small (two- to four-inch) minnows better than larger baits.

Fly-Fishing for River Walleyes

Walleyes on fly-fishing tackle? Well, yes, as a matter of fact, it has happened. Several times I've actually had walleyes take flies when I was fishing for smallmouth bass. This is not to say that I'm advocating such an approach on a serious level, but be advised that it does occur. Of the dozen or so walleyes I've caught on a fly rod, all but one have taken a crayfish fly fished right on the bottom. Crayfish are a favorite forage of the river walleye and if you fish crayfish patterns in areas known to hold walleyes you might be pleasantly surprised.

Walleyes are one of my favorite gamefish, and if you are fishing one of the rivers that have walleyes and are able to land a few of the fish, I'm sure they will become one of your favorites, too.

NINE

Channel Catfish

Several species of catfish are found in the rivers of the mid-Atlantic states, including channel cats, flatheads, and bullheads. The most popular is the channel catfish, which is found in all of the rivers. The larger flathead is found in the New and Greenbrier rivers, but since it has only a limited range, we will concentrate on the channel cat, although the techniques we cover should also work for the flatheads. The bullhead catfish is not a gamefish species many people go after.

Channel cats may well be the second most popular fish with anglers, behind the smallmouth bass. Channel cats are found in good numbers, are fairly easy to locate and catch, and, as many fishermen will tell you, they are the best tasting of the fish found in the rivers.

Channel cats like moving waters, and are often found in large numbers below the many dams on the rivers. If the dam was built for hydroelectric purposes, so much the better, for when the water is drawn through the generators, a large number of baitfish will be drawn through also, and the result is nothing less than a smorgasbord of ground-up fish that attracts channel cats from long distances.

BIOLOGICAL INFORMATION

The channel cat is primarily a bottom feeder, and it is well equipped for that role. Its main distinguishing characteristic is its long whiskers or barbels that allow it to detect and identify underwater odors from very long distances. This highly developed sense of smell also allows catfish to find food in murky or muddy water conditions and at night, when other gamefish, which rely more on their sight, may be at a disadvantage.

There are several physical characteristics that separate the channel cat from other members of the catfish family. The easiest method of identification is to observe the tail of the fish. On the channel catfish, it is deeply forked and each fork comes to a sharp point. On the bullhead and flathead, the tail is squared or rounded, and lacks the fork found on the channel cat.

The channel catfish spawns in the spring, usually during the month of May when the water temperature is in the mid-60s; after the eggs have hatched, the male will guard the young for several weeks. On many occasions, I have observed a black ball of young catfish along the shoreline and, by looking the area over closely, was able to spot the male lurking nearby.

AVERAGE SIZES AND TROPHY FISH

The average channel cat caught by anglers would probably range between ten and fifteen inches in length, and for most anglers this is fine, because cats of this size are just right for eating purposes. However, much larger channel cats are caught in these rivers, and a trophy fish would probably be a channel cat weighing more than ten pounds.

Flatheads grow much larger—they may reach a weight of forty or more pounds. On the New and Greenbrier rivers, flatheads weighing more than twenty pounds aren't uncommon.

TACKLE FOR CATFISH

The tackle used for catfishing is usually heavier than that used for bass or walleyes. This is necessary because the cats are often taken in waters with heavy currents that require the angler to use a lot of weight to keep the bait on the bottom.

However, if you are wading and casting lightly weighted baits to little pockets or eddy areas, you can use lighter tackle, which will allow you to enjoy the fight of the fish more.

When wading for catfish, I like a medium-weight spinning outfit, loaded with eight- or ten-pound-test line. This type of fishing usually means casting light baits with only a split shot or two for additional weight, and spinning tackle is better suited for this purpose.

I do most of my catfishing out of an anchored boat, and use a medium-weight bait-casting outfit with ten- or twelve-pound-test line. With a fairly stiff rod, you can handle up to a half-ounce weight and a big bait, and ten-pound-test will handle any catfish you hook if you do your part well.

This angler is anchored and fishing for catfish on the Shenandoah River.

BAITS AND TECHNIQUES

Catfish will hit a wide variety of baits, alive or dead. Over the years, stories about the tendency of the catfish to prefer dead and, in fact, rotten forage have abounded, but most experienced river fishermen know that a live minnow or nightcrawler is probably as good as any stink bait you can use.

Other favorite baits would include cut bait (chunks of rough fish such as suckers or fallfish), shrimp, chicken livers, and the store-bought stink baits, which are an unsavory blend of various animal parts that I would rather not speculate about.

Over the years, I've tried a number of different baits, but really haven't found anything better than chicken livers, minnows, and cut bait—preferably a chunk of fallfish. In the springtime, especially after spring rains, nightcrawlers are hard to beat, and at times shrimp seem to be better than anything else. But my experience has been that you really don't need those gosh-awful commercial stink baits.

The key to catfishing, just as in any other type of fishing, is to find the fish, and then find a way of presenting the bait to them. This means adapting your tackle and approach according to the water.

For example, one of the most popular catfishing spots in Maryland is below Conowingo Dam on the Susquehanna River. The power company built a fishermen's catwalk on the dam, which allows people to fish straight down into the water being released when the plant is generating.

This is a tremendous catfishing spot. The water is filled with ground-up fish and catfish thrive in such a spot. The only problem is that to get the bait down to the fish, you must use a heavy weight—and heavy tackle to handle the heavy weight. Most of the catwalk regulars use tackle you would normally see in saltwater fishing situations.

Now compare this to another favorite catfishing spot, the Potomac River near Harpers Ferry, West Virginia. This part of the river is filled with rock ledges and other formations and, although the waters are

Captain Earl Ashenfelter with a nice channel cat from the Susquehanna River.

swift and treacherous, it can be waded in most areas. Fishermen like to cast lightly weighted baits to the pools behind the rock formations, and most use relatively light tackle.

Here you have two totally different types of fishing for the same gamefish. At the Conowingo Dam catwalk, the light tackle preferred by the Harpers Ferry regulars would be almost useless, and at Harpers Ferry the heavy equipment needed at Conowingo would be out of place in the hands of wading fishermen.

DAY OR NIGHT?

There is considerable disagreement on which is the best time to catch catfish. Some say that to really do well, you have to fish at night, while others say that you can catch all the catfish you want in the daytime.

There's no doubt about the fact that catfish are somewhat nocturnal in their habits. However, the key point to remember is that catfish, and almost any other fish for that matter, are opportunists, and they aren't likely to pass up an easy meal, day or night. When the gates open on a dam, and the water is filled with pieces of freshly ground fish, the cats could care less about the time of day; all they know is that the dinner bell has rung.

The biggest difference between day and night is that the fish seem to move around more at night, and they can be caught in shallower water. I've fished many spots that are tremendous at night, but don't hold fish during the day because they are shallow, and the fish would feel too exposed there during the daylight hours.

Butch Ward of Clear Spring, Maryland, is one of the best catfishermen I've met and enjoys considerable success fishing during the day. Butch knows that the fish tend to hole up during the day, but he also knows they will feed if you can find them.

Ward has caught some very impressive stringers of catfish from the upper Potomac by fishing deep holes where the fish gather in large numbers. Most of the better holes are eight or more feet deep, and feature cover in the form of underwater rock formations or downed trees. His favorite baits are big chub minnows, and he says that sometimes the fish want them alive, and at other times they seem to prefer them dead. But the key, according to Butch, is to find the deepest hole in a given section of river and you will usually find the cats holding there during the daylight hours.

Butch Ward lands a catfish while carefully avoiding getting pierced by pectoral fins.

For some reason, the channel cat doesn't enjoy the popularity with many fishermen that it deserves. However, for those in the know, the catfish is a favorite quarry, and when the fishing is over, there's nothing better than a plate of deep-fried catfish, surrounded by hush puppies and cole slaw.

TEN

Muskellunge

Few gamefish enjoy the mystique or glamour of the muskellunge or, as it is usually called, muskie. When you look at the physical character-istics of the fish, and consider the fact a mature specimen will be be-tween thirty and forty-five inches long, and may weigh as much as thirty to forty pounds, you can understand why anglers seem to regard muskies with a certain degree of awe.

Not only is a muskie big, but it also features an impressive head on its streamlined body, with a mouthful of very sharp teeth. For the freshwater angler, the muskie is the ultimate predator, the fish at the very top of the food chain, the baddest dude in the river.

Few anglers, or even biologists, understand the fish well. They tend to be basically loners, it is thought; solitary predators, they usu-ally stake out a territory and wait to grab unsuspecting prey from am-bush sites. In the rivers discussed in this book, that would mean in the deeper pools where they take advantage of such cover as downed trees or underwater rock formations.

Muskies are notorious for being selective feeders at times, but, on the other hand, they have been documented as feeding on nearly ev-erything edible found in the river. Favorite foods include some of the rough fish, such as redhorse suckers, white suckers, fallfish, and small carp. Gamefish such as the smallmouth bass would be eaten if they strayed within striking range. A friend who fishes the Susquehanna River had an estimated twenty-pounder strike and take an eight-inch bass that he had hooked and was reeling in on light spinning tackle. As he described it, the fish loomed up from the bottom of the pool like a creature out of a movie, ate the bass, and cut his light line all in one motion.

Muskies will also eat reptiles such as water snakes, and have the reputation of being quite fond of baby ducks. In short, if it's alive and moving, it's subject to being eaten if a fish is on the feed.

BIOLOGICAL INFORMATION

Both purebred and tiger muskies are found in many of the rivers. The hybrid tiger is cultured by taking eggs from a female muskie and fertilizing them with sperm from the male northern pike. The resulting fish is mostly muskie, and there seems to be a good case for switching over to the hybrids, from a hatchery manager's standpoint, because they show superior growth rates when young, and the survival rate of young is said to be better than that of purebred muskies. In addition, biologists report that tiger muskies will feed on food pellets while in the hatchery environment, whereas purebreds want real live minnows as feed. This, of course, makes raising tiger muskies cheaper for fisheries managers, both in terms of food costs and in terms of the labor required to maintain the fish.

Since the tiger is a hybrid, it shows signs of what biologists call "hybrid vigor" (which means it is a more vigorous fish than the purebreds), and is more of a wanderer, searching the water for food. For this reason some say the tiger may be easier for the angler to fool, but even considering that, you will seldom meet an angler who catches a lot of muskies—tigers or purebreds.

In most rivers, the muskie population is maintained by stocking young fish (usually fingerlings) from hatcheries. There does seem to be limited reproduction in some rivers, but the fish do not appear to be capable of maintaining viable populations without help from stocking programs.

AVERAGE SIZES AND TROPHY FISH

The average muskie caught by anglers is large by other river fish standards. Even one that a diehard muskie angler would consider small would be a very big fish to most weekend bass fishermen. If there were such a thing as an average, it would be somewhere between eight and fourteen pounds, since most mature fish are in that weight area. However, in the James, New, Susquehanna, and even the little Juniata River, much larger fish are available.

The muskie specialist (and that's what most successful muskie anglers are) is looking for bigger game. Trophy fish would be muskies weighing twenty pounds or more, and in the Susquehanna, Juniata, James, and New rivers, catching a muskie of this size is quite feasible.

*Trophy muskie landed from the Spring-
wood section of the James River. Photo
courtesy Bill Cochran*

If you are willing to set your sights high, a muskie of thirty pounds
or more is possible in the rivers, and such a fish would be an outstanding trophy by any standard. But in most cases, anglers consider any
fish over twenty pounds a trophy fish when taken from one of these
rivers.

TACKLE FOR MUSKIES

Most muskies hooked each year are probably incidental catches.
Notice I said hooked—not landed. The average angler, floating a river
and fishing for bass and panfish, would not be well enough equipped to
handle a twenty-five-pound muskie if one decided to give his lure a shot.

Serious muskie fishing requires serious tackle. When you are after
fish weighing up to thirty pounds you will need tackle that can handle
the strain of a heavy fish. Compounding the problem is the fact that the
sharp teeth of a muskie can easily cut through even fairly heavy monofilament during the course of a struggle.

The ideal muskie outfit for casting would be a heavy bait-casting rig, featuring a 5½- to 6½-foot rod. Your reel should be loaded with seventeen- to thirty-pound-test mono that has a short shock leader of very heavy monofilament or, better yet, a braided wire leader.

Many anglers don't use a shock leader of monofilament or a wire leader and still catch and land muskies, but you are bucking the odds if you imitate them, particularly when you consider the number of hours it may take to entice a muskie to strike.

I asked Lefty Kreh what rig he would use if muskies were the quarry, and he recommended the following. (Lefty has fished all over the world for toothy gamefish in both fresh and salt water, and has also written a book with Mark Sosin titled *Practical Fishing Knots* on fishing rigs and knots.)

Starting with a heavy monofilament of seventeen- to twenty-pound test, attach a barrel swivel. The barrel swivel can be connected to the line with your favorite knot, such as a Palamar or an improved cinch knot. To the other end of the barrel swivel attach eight inches of thirty-pound-test stainless steel braided wire. Use a figure-eight knot to attach the wire to the terminal end of the barrel knot. To the other end of the wire, attach a heavy-duty snap such as the one made by Crossloc. The snap should be attached using another figure-eight knot. The lure or baited hook is then secured to the rig with the snap.

Lefty said that there are other knots that may used when working with wire leaders, but the figure-eight is one of the easiest to master.

FISHING METHODS

When I think of muskie fishing, I think of a line from an article I once read. I can't remember the name of the magazine, or the writer, but the quote from an old-time muskie angler stayed with me. When asked to name the best time to fish for muskie, the expert said, "The two best times to fish are when it's raining, and when it's not."

This statement, as silly as it might sound to many, says something about the fish and the anglers who pursue them. Muskie fishing requires a dedication that few anglers possess, and even the most successful fishermen fish hours and hours for each fish landed. One of the maddening things about muskie behavior is that they might refuse or follow a lure several times before they finally take it.

There are three principal ways of catching muskies in rivers: casting lures, trolling lures, and fishing live bait. Each method has its proponents, and each can be successful at a given time.

Muskie expert Tim McCoy prefers trolling in the Whitehorn section of the New River. Photo courtesy Bill Cochran

The casting method involves throwing large lures, such as big crankbaits, large floating/diving lures, spinners, or jigs to spots known to hold muskies, or that you suspect hold muskies. As mentioned earlier, the fish generally hold in the deeper pools, often near underwater rock formations where they wait to ambush prey.

In many areas trolling is the preferred method and the system does offer the advantage of covering a lot of water and keeping the lure in the water for long periods.

You can also fish with live bait, either by drifting the bait near the bottom of a pool, or by anchoring near a suspected muskie lair and letting the bait swim near the suspected muskie position. The bait should be a large one—suckers six to eight inches long are the preferred bait. Large chubs can also be used.

During the early spring, muskies will often concentrate near the mouths of small streams, feeding on the suckers that are gathering to ascend the streams to spawn. This usually occurs from mid-February to mid-March. The suckers will form in large schools, waiting for a rain to raise the creeks to make the passage upstream easier. During this period the shorebound angler can do quite well, since the fish will be near the shore, and often up into the small creek itself.

A favorite technique on the Juniata is to drive from stream to stream, fishing each spot for a few minutes, then moving on to the next incoming stream. Favorite lures for this include large crankbaits in a silver- or perch-colored finish, spoons, or the long (four- or five-inch) curlytailed grubs. Several Juniata regulars report that the white grub seems to attract the most muskies. This is one of the few times when you might find a concentration of muskies, and be lucky enough to catch more than one fish from the same general area.

Muskies are a wonderful gamefish. They grow to reach very large sizes, they strike both artificial lures and live bait, and they feed actively in nearly all water temperatures, which means year-round fishing opportunities.

Few anglers really understand the fish well, but this only seems to heighten the challenge for the diehard muskie fisherman.

ELEVEN

Carp

A carp is likely to be the biggest fish most anglers will catch from the rivers of the mid-Atlantic. For most people, it's an exciting encounter. Carp will hit a wide variety of baits, and put up a strong and determined battle once hooked.

Carp aren't native to these rivers; for that matter, they aren't native to this country. Carp were first introduced to the rivers in the 1800s and, since they are extremely adaptable fish, have flourished.

Carp spawn in the early summer when the water temperature reaches the high 60s. When these fish move into the shallows to spawn, they create quite a ruckus, splashing and thrashing against aquatic vegetation and submerged timber as they attach their eggs, which are covered with a sticky substance, to underwater objects.

AVERAGE SIZES AND TROPHY FISH

Carp grow fast, and one weighing less than ten pounds is small. Most fisherman who go after carp on a regular basis consider a twenty-pounder a big carp, and anything over twenty pounds is a real brute when caught on fairly light tackle.

Each of the rivers produces carp weighing twenty pounds or more and when you hook your first twenty-pounder it will give you a battle you won't likely forget.

TACKLE FOR CARP

Since carp are big, strong fish, many serious anglers use very heavy tackle that allows them to overpower the fish. However, you can have a lot of fun while carp fishing by using fairly light tackle and playing the fish instead of horsing it in.

Consider the following: Back in 1973, my wife and I were living in Great Falls, Montana. We were there at the request of the U.S. Air

Force. The Air Force called it active duty—I called it paid vacation in a sportsman's paradise.

At any rate, I was fishing the Missouri River, not far from where we lived, and was using an ultralight spinning outfit loaded with four-pound-test line, and a Mepps Spinner. On one of the first casts of the day, I had a hard strike, and the drag on the little spinning reel buzzed as a very big fish headed downriver.

To make a long story short, this was one of the longest fights I've ever been involved in, and I was sure that I had hooked the biggest trout in Montana. Finally, after following the fish up and down the river for over an hour, I was able to get a look at it, and was very unhappy to find that I was attached to a carp weighing ten or twelve pounds.

As I beached the fish, muttering unprintable words about the luck involved in catching a carp on a spinner in one of the best trout rivers in the West, an elderly gentleman walked over and asked what was wrong.

When I explained the situation, he told me something that I'll never forget. "Boy," he said, "I don't see what your problem is. That carp just gave you a longer and better fight than any trout you'll ever catch. Now, if you don't eat carp, release that fish so someone else can enjoy catching him some day."

I did release the fish, and over the years, I've thought of that gentleman on many occasions. He made some very good points, the most important being, in my mind, that any fish caught on sporting tackle can provide the angler with a great fishing experience.

While I don't recommend ultralight tackle for carp, I do recommend a medium-weight outfit, with eight-, ten-, or twelve-pound-test line. It can be spinning or bait-casting tackle with a 5½- or 6-foot rod and matching reel. I now use bait-casting tackle, but for years caught big carp on spinning tackle and had a ball doing it. You won't be able to horse big carp with such tackle, but you can land even the biggest ones if you do your job well.

BAITS FOR CARP

Biologists will tell you that carp are omnivorous feeders; that is, they eat both plants and animals. Fishermen who fish for carp will tell you that carp eat anything and everything.

However, there are certain baits that seem to attract carp better than anything else. The most common bait is a doughball of some sort.

*Carp give young anglers the opportunity to learn
how to play big fish. Matthew Price had a lot of
fun landing this carp while fishing the Potomac
River near Brunswick, Md.*

Some fishermen use highly secret recipes for making their doughballs, while others take the easy way out, making do with common breakfast cereals like oatmeal and shredded wheat. I take the easy way myself.

Oatmeal is a proven carp catcher and a very easy bait to use. You simply take a handful of oatmeal, dip your hand into the river, wetting the oatmeal, and squeeze it into a ball. Shredded wheat works the same way. Both breakfast cereals form hard doughballs that stay on the hook well, and both will catch carp under most conditions.

Recently, I was looking over some scientifically conducted tests on the scenting capabilities of fish. I noticed that carp were used in the experiment, and that one of the scents that was very attractive to them was strawberry. This is no surprise to many Potomac River carp fishermen because they have been using doughballs laced with strawberry Jell-O for years now.

Lefty Kreh, who fishes all over the world and is one of the few bona fide experts on virtually every type of sportfishing, is also a great carp-fishing fan. Lefty has a proven recipe for carp dough.

KREH'S CARP DOUGH
1 pint water
Half of a 3-ounce package of strawberry Jell-O
1 tbs. vanilla extract
1 tbs. sugar
2 cups cornmeal
1 cup flour

In a saucepan, bring water to boil and add Jell-O, vanilla, and sugar. Stir for a minute and then reduce heat so that mixture barely boils. In a bowl, combine cornmeal and flour and mix well with a spoon. Sprinkle some of the cornmeal/flour mixture on the surface of the water. The bubbles from the boiling mixture will make volcanolike eruptions through the cornmeal and flour. As the eruptions occur, cover them with more of the cornmeal and flour mixture until it is used up, then stir for 30 seconds. Remove from stove and let cool. Mold the dough into balls about two-thirds the size of a golf ball and either use immediately or store in the refrigerator for up to three days. Makes approximately 30 doughballs.

According to Lefty, this doughball is gummy and tough, which makes it easy to keep on the hook, and features the strawberry scent which carp really go for.

In the springtime, especially right after spring rains, night-crawlers are a very good carp bait; and several of my friends use kernels of canned corn with good success. I've also accidentally caught carp on live minnows, cut bait intended for catfish, crayfish (both live crayfish and crayfish flies intended for bass), jigs, and crankbaits. As we noted at the beginning, carp eat almost everything.

Carp don't enjoy a very good reputation with many anglers. Perhaps this is because they aren't considered a very good table fish. Also, the bottom-grubbing tendencies of carp turn many fishermen off. But like them or not, carp are here to stay; they can provide plenty of action and are a lot of fun to catch, when taken on light tackle.

TWELVE

Panfish

The generic term *panfish* applies to a number of the smaller fish found in the rivers. Usually they are members of the sunfish family. Some of the more common include the redear sunfish, pumpkinseed, bluegill, green sunfish, crappies, and the rock bass (or, as they are often called, goggle-eye).

In terms of overall popularity, the panfish would have to rank quite high. The fish often school in large numbers and, once located, always seem willing to strike either live bait or small artificial lures.

Young anglers are probably the biggest fans of panfish angling, since the key word with kids is action, and the fact that their catch may not be the biggest fish in the river is of little significance.

Panfish of all species have several traits in common. They are usually found in schools or groups; they are most often found near some type of cover that will protect them from the large predators in the river; and they all eat a wide variety of food. Favorite panfish foods include insects, small minnows, crayfish, worms—nearly anything organic that is small enough to get into their mouths.

TACKLE AND FISHING TECHNIQUES

The tackle for panfishing should be light. An ultralight spinning or spin-casting outfit with four- to six-pound-test line is ideal. The rod action should be quite springy, to allow the angler to enjoy the fight of the smaller fish. And don't underestimate the little fish—inch for inch, they are among the hardest fighters in the river.

Fly-fishing for panfish is always fun, and can be an excellent way to introduce the young or novice angler to the sport. The redear sunfish is an active surface feeder and will take small popping bugs with gusto. Almost all of these fish will take small underwater flies, such as nymphs and tiny streamers, and when the angler scales down to lighter-weight outfits, such as you would use for trout, the fishing can be quite sporty.

TYPES OF PANFISH

Rock Bass

The rock bass is one of the more prevalent of the panfish, and one of the sportiest. This little fish is known by many names, including goggle-eye and redeye. The rock bass is a river and stream fish and prefers to hide in rocky areas typical of excellent smallmouth waters. Its scientific name, *Ambloplites rupestris,* is Latin for "of the rocks."

In many sections of the rivers, the rock bass will be the most frequent panfish catch simply because more fishermen are after smallmouth bass and the rock bass is found in exactly the same areas. They even spawn in similar areas, at about the same water temperatures (62 to 70 degrees), and the male rock bass vigorously guards the nest, causing many to be hooked by fishermen who are after bass in the spring.

After the spawn, the rock bass tend to scatter to areas with cover, but continue to share much of their habitat with the smallmouth, eating small minnows, crayfish, worms, and insects. Although members of

Rock bass are among the most abundant of the pan-fish, and readily strike many different lures and flies. This fish took a hellgramite fly.

the panfish group, the rock bass has a larger mouth than most panfish and can take larger baits and lures. Small crankbaits, spinners, and underwater flies will usually fool a few rock bass if they are present in the area. One point to note, however, is that they don't seem to feed on the surface as much as the redear or the bluegill, and fly rod poppers usually aren't as effective as underwater flies.

Crappie

In certain areas, you can find crappies in the rivers. Crappies are usually a lake fish, but have found certain sections of the rivers suitable. Most of the time, the crappies will be found in slower, deeper pools, or in slack-water areas behind dams. Crappies are a very cover-oriented fish, and when found in the rivers will nearly always be holding on some type of underwater cover, such as a downed tree or fallen bridge pilings.

Crappies are primarily minnow eaters, and when they've been located the best lure is usually a small, brightly colored jig. Small marabou jigs or three-inch curlytail grubs are usually the best artificial lures. Live bait fans can usually take crappies with very small minnows fished near the holding cover.

Panfish are a favorite with youngsters. This pair got a stringer of panfish while wading near weed beds.

Sunfish

The sunfish, such as the redear, bluegill, and pumpkinseed, will most often be found holding near some cover, such as a weed bed, boat dock, or fallen tree. The sunfish will take certain live baits such as worms or hellgramites readily, but are less inclined to eat minnows. Young anglers like to watch a bobber and this is a good way to present a wriggling garden worm to a school of sunfish.

The panfish are an important part of the overall fishing opportunities present in the rivers. Many anglers find the members of the sunfish family particularly good eating, and many younger anglers use their early encounters with panfish to develop skills that prepare them to take on the bigger game found in the rivers.

THIRTEEN

The Potomac River

The stately Potomac is often referred to as the Nation's River. This seems entirely appropriate, since it is a river that has always played an important role in our national history.

The huge tidal river that meanders past the Lincoln Memorial and the Washington Monument in Washington, D.C., can be traced to small streams that begin in the mountains of West Virginia and Virginia.

The North Branch, which is approximately ninety-seven miles long, has its origins near Fairfax Stone, West Virginia. Over the years, the North Branch has suffered greatly from the effects of mining acids that were allowed to leach into its waters. For a long time the river was considered sterile—unable to support most forms of aquatic life. However, in recent years this trend has been reversed and the long-term prospects for the North Branch look encouraging.

The South Branch of the Potomac begins near Hightown, Virginia, and is a first-rate fishery for most of its length, important enough to warrant separate treatment in chapter 19. The South Branch runs for approximately 132 miles before converging with the North Branch near Oldtown, Maryland. The upper part of the South Branch is considered a fine trout stream; the lower section of the river offers excellent fishing for smallmouth bass, panfish, and channel catfish.

The section of the Potomac that we will be looking at runs from the confluence of the North Branch and the South Branch, downstream to the area called the Potomac River Breaks, above the Great Falls.

This is a part of the country that will appeal to nature lovers and history buffs. As the river makes its way through the mountains of the Oldtown–to–Hancock area, and into the farmlands that are typical of the Williamsport–to–Great Falls section, it will pass many areas rich in historical significance: places like the famous Antietam Battlefield near Sharpsburg, the site of the single bloodiest day of fighting in the Civil War, and Harpers Ferry, where John Brown led his famous, though ill-fated, raid on the Federal Armory in 1859.

Along the way, you are likely to see many forms of wildlife. Deer, turkey, beaver, waterfowl, and osprey are common sights. And in certain sections, bald eagles have found the river a suitable place to raise a family, and make yearly visits to nest near its waters.

GAMEFISH OF THE POTOMAC

Smallmouth Bass

Smallmouths are found throughout the section of the Potomac we are looking at here, and are the most popular fish with anglers. In most sections of the river, the average angler has the opportunity to catch thirty or more smallmouths per day, ranging in size from a few inches to five pounds or more.

In 1979, the Maryland Department of Natural Resources raised the minimum legal keeper size on Potomac smallmouths from nine to twelve inches. This came about with support, and perhaps as a result of pressure, from sportsmen's groups.

Many anglers feel that this change in regulations was beneficial to the smallmouths. They say they can remember the time when fishermen fishing for the table had a hard time catching a few smallmouths that would make the nine-inch minimum length. Now the average smallmouth is nine inches or more in length.

Fly casting to smallmouth near Brunswick.

Largemouth Bass

The sections of the Potomac that we will be looking at are primarily smallmouth bass habitat; however, there are certain sections that usually harbor a few largemouths.

The slack-water areas behind dams, particularly the Big Slackwater section behind Dam #4 near Williamsport, is a noted largemouth bass area, and the Whites Ferry and Seneca areas are also known to hold good populations of largemouths.

Although largemouths aren't the principal gamefish in the Potomac, the river does produce some exceptional fish. There have been several largemouths weighing more than six pounds taken from the Edwards Ferry area of the river.

Walleye

The 1979 stocking of walleyes in the Potomac marks one of the outstanding programs in Maryland's management of its warm water fisheries.

The walleyes were stocked as fingerlings and fry, and found the river very much to their liking. Growth rates have been very good, and walleyes weighing more than seven pounds have been taken from the river.

From as early as 1984, biologists have found that the walleyes are successfully spawning in the river, and it is hoped that the walleye fishery will eventually become self-sustaining, and that stocking will not be necessary.

As of this time, most of the walleyes stocked in the Potomac have been released in the section starting at Dam #5 near Williamsport, downstream to the area near the Dargan Bend landing.

Catfish

The channel cat may be the second most popular gamefish on the Potomac, and many areas of the river are popular with catfishermen. The best spots for channel cats are swift-water areas that also offer underwater rocks or other cover for the fish. The waters below the standing dams are very good for catfish; below Dam #5 and Dam #4 they are quite productive.

Carp

Carp are quite abundant throughout the river, but seem more plentiful in the middle river, from Dam #5 downstream. Some of the biggest carp come from the river below Harpers Ferry, where the Potomac becomes

Boyd Pfeiffer lands a nice walleye from below Dam #4.

wider after being joined by the Shenandoah. Carp weighing more than twenty pounds are not uncommon in the river.

Panfish
Panfish such as redear sunfish, pumpkinseed sunfish, and rock bass are found in the river in large numbers, and in some of the slower sections behind Dam #4 and Dam #5 you can sometimes find crappies. Panfish don't have the following of some of the other fish, but the little fighters have often saved the day when the bass, walleyes, or other more popular fish weren't biting.

Muskie
Officially, muskies aren't found in the Potomac. That is, the state fisheries managers haven't pursued a muskie stocking program and my conversations with them have indicated that they feel the Potomac is not the proper type of water for a muskie fishery. In fact, Maryland is the only state without a muskie stocking program. The fish are in the Potomac, however, and are showing up in sufficient numbers to make them worthy of mention.

The exact source of the muskies in the Potomac remains a mystery to most of us, but theories range from fish being washed out of other streams and ponds near the river, to unauthorized stocking of young fish by fishermen. Whatever the source, muskies ranging from twelve to fifteen pounds are being caught each season—mostly by accident, and mostly by people who are fishing for bass. At this time, catching a muskie in the river is possible, but must still be considered a rarity.

ACCESS TO THE RIVER

Public access to the Potomac is excellent because most of the Maryland shore of the river is owned by the federal government as part of the Chesapeake and Ohio (C&O) Canal National Historical Park. The park service not only maintains the canal towpath, which is a very popular hiking and biking path that is enjoyed by thousands, but also maintains boat-launching ramps that provide excellent access for fishermen.

On the West Virginia and Virginia shores, the land is nearly all privately owned, and access to this land requires the permission of a landowner, which it may or may not be possible to get. There is, however, a West Virginia Department of Natural Resources ramp on the West Virginia shore in Shepherdstown.

The Potomac is unusual in that Maryland owns the entire river right up to the high water mark (an ambiguous description that few seem to understand) on the opposite shore. In most instances where a river forms the boundary between two states, each state owns its half of the river, but the Potomac belongs to Maryland.

The one important legal note on this matter is that fishermen holding valid West Virginia or Virginia fishing licenses can legally fish the Potomac, but must observe all pertinent Maryland rules and regulations, such as minimum size requirements and creel limits.

Selected Sections of the River

Section I. Spring Gap, Md., to Hancock, Md.
Back-in Ramps

1. Spring Gap, C&O Canal National Historical Park (NHP), off Md. Rt. 51.

2. Fifteenmile Creek ramp, C&O Canal NHP, at Little Orleans, Md.

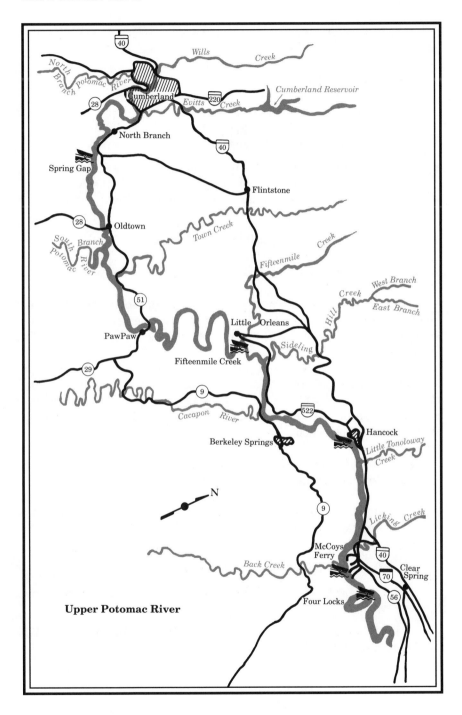

Upper Potomac River

  3. Little Tonoloway ramp, C&O Canal NHP, mouth of Little
     Tonoloway Creek, Hancock, Md.

Suggested Float Trips

  1. Spring Gap to Oldtown, 7 miles
     Put-in: Spring Gap ramp, C&O Canal NHP, off Md. Rt. 51
     Take-out: Toll bridge across river at Oldtown, Md.

  2. Fifteenmile Creek to Dam #6 remnants, 7.5 miles
     Put-in: Fifteenmile Creek ramp, at Little Orleans, Md.
     Take-out: Dam #6 remnants, off Woodmont Road, southwest of
     Hancock.

  3. Dam #6 remnants to Hancock, 9.1 miles
     Put-in: Dam #6 (described above)
     Take-out: Hancock C&O Canal NHP ramp, Town of Hancock.

This section of the Potomac is as scenic as any section of any of the
rivers covered. The river is narrow and winding, and much of the
shoreline is undeveloped. It's one of the very nicest boating areas for
scenic beauty.

This section can be quite shallow during the summer months, and
although boat ramps are available, most anglers use them only during
the spring and fall when the river has more water in it. During the
summer, plan on wading or using a shallow-draft boat or canoe for
floating from pool to pool.

Section II. Hancock, Md., to Williamsport, Md.
Back-in Boat Ramps

  1. Little Tonoloway ramp, C&O Canal NHP, mouth of Little
     Tonoloway Creek, Hancock, Md.

  2. McCoys Ferry ramp, C&O Canal NHP, McCoys Ferry Road,
     off Md. Rt. 56 near Big Pool, Md.

  3. Four Locks ramp, C&O Canal NHP, off Md. Rt. 56 near Big
     Spring, Md.

  4. Williamsport ramp, C&O Canal NHP, Riverbottom Park, Wil-
     liamsport, Md.

Biologist Ed Enamait with a nice Potomac smallmouth.

Suggested Float Trips

1. Hancock to McCoys Ferry, 14.1 miles (*Note:* This is one of the longest trips recommended, but can be completed in one day if you move through the shallow areas, and fish only the better water.)
   Put-in: Little Tonoloway ramp, C&O Canal NHP, Town of Hancock.
   Take-out: McCoys Ferry ramp, C&O Canal NHP, McCoys Ferry Road, off Md. Rt. 56, near Big Pool.

2. Dam #5 to Williamsport, 6.7 miles
   Put-in: Dam #5 parking area, Dam #5 road, near Clear Spring.
   Take-out: Williamsport C&O Canal NHP ramp, Town of Williamsport, just downstream from US Rt. 11 bridge over river.

Hancock marks the beginning of the end of the mountainous setting as the river starts entering into the piedmont section. This is one of the more productive sections in terms of smallmouth bass and, though the water gets low in the summer, the local boaters can usually run the river between Hancock and McCoys Ferry even in the summer months.

The Hancock–to–McCoys float is one of my favorites, but it is a long float at low-water levels. McCoys Ferry ramp marks the beginning of a seven-mile stretch of impounded deep water behind Dam #5. This stretch can be quite productive to fish, and is more like a lake type of environment. But be aware that during the summer, and particularly on weekends, the section is polluted with large pleasure boats that usually launch at Four Locks, some pulling water skiers, and others just acting like fools with high-powered machines that belong on the Chesapeake Bay or, better yet, San Francisco Bay. Many seem to take particular pleasure in disturbing fishermen in small boats. You get the picture.

The area below Dam #5 is excellent for catfish, smallmouth, and carp. Extending from the Maryland shore is a series of rocks that run parallel to the dam and reach nearly across the river. This is an excellent opportunity for anglers without boats. At normal flows you can follow the rocks out into the river and cast back toward the dam. I know, because I grew up fishing off those rocks and only live about one mile from them now.

The Dam #5–to–Williamsport float is a good bet. The carry-in point at Dam #5 is down a steep bank, however, so a light boat is needed.

Section III. Williamsport, Md., to Dargan Bend ramp
Back-in Boat Ramps

1. Big Slackwater ramp, C&O Canal NHP, off Dam #4 road, near Williamsport, Md.

2. Taylors Landing boat ramp, C&O Canal NHP, off Taylors Landing Road, north of Sharpsburg, Md.

3. Snyders Landing boat ramp, C&O Canal NHP, Snyders Landing Road, Sharpsburg, Md.

4. Shepherdstown ramp, West Virginia Department of Natural Resources, below Md. Rt. 34 bridge, Town of Shepherdstown, W.Va.

Author with a big smallmouth taken on a fall float trip.

5. Dargan Bend ramp, C&O Canal NHP, off Harpers Ferry Road, south of Sharpsburg, Md.

Suggested Float Trips

1. Dam #4 to Snyders Landing, 7.6 miles
   Put-in: Dam #4 parking lot, Dam #4 road, south of Williamsport.
   Take-out: Snyders Landing C&O Canal NHP ramp, Snyders Landing Road, Sharpsburg, Md.

2. Shepherdstown to Dargan Bend, 7.1 miles
   Put-in: Shepherdstown, W.Va. DNR ramp, just below Md. Rt. 34 ramp over river, Town of Shepherdstown, W.Va.
   Take-out: Dargan Bend C&O Canal NHP ramp, off Harpers Ferry Road, south of Sharpsburg.

The entire area from below Dam #4 to Dargan Bend is prime smallmouth, walleye, and channel cat water. My favorite method of fishing the section below the dam is to put in at Taylors Landing and

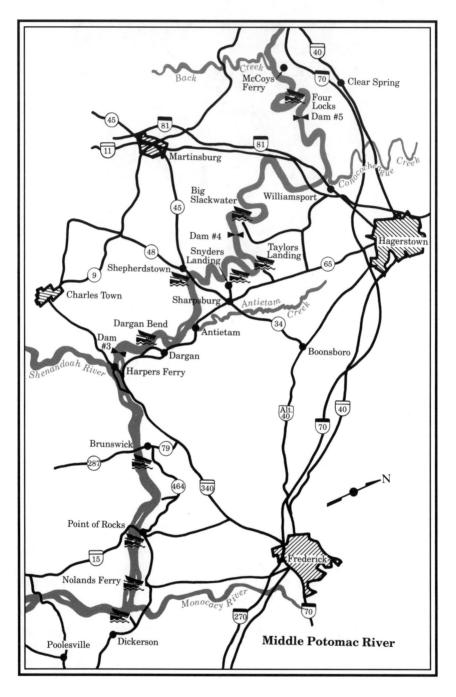

Middle Potomac River

run upstream to the dam. This is tricky boating during normal flow, with plenty of rock ledges and fish pots to navigate.

The area below Dam #4, downstream to Snyders Landing, is popular wading water. About one mile upstream from Snyders Landing is a series of ledges running parallel with the river, called the Horsebacks, that is used by many people for wade-fishing.

From Snyders Landing downstream to Shepherdstown, the river is generally deeper, and this is one of the few sections that can consistently be boated without the boat having to be dragged over shallow areas. There are still plenty of shallow areas to watch out for, however.

Just below Shepherdstown is a series of riffles, called Packhorse Fords, which is one of the most popular wet wading areas on the river for smallmouth and channel catfish. There are some very nice pools and water pockets below the riffles. The entire section is excellent for floating in a shallow-draft boat, but the section from Snyders Landing to Shepherdstown features some slow-moving water that can cause a problem if you are fighting an upstream wind.

Section IV. The Harpers Ferry Area

You won't see any float trips for this section because I don't recommend boating the river from the remnants of Dam #3 downstream to below Knoxville. This is an area very popular with canoeists and others, but is considered dangerous water for those who are not white-water boaters.

You can fish the area below Dam #3 where there is excellent wading for smallmouths and channel cats. When I was in high school, my biology teacher and I would wade this area for catfish, using groundhog liver as bait. Naturally, to obtain the groundhog liver for bait, we also had to go groundhog hunting, which was an altogether acceptable deal from my point of view.

This is very productive water for fishermen, but you should carefully note the following: This is tricky water to wade. There is a significant current to fight, and the bottom is quite irregular, with drop-offs, swirls, and back currents that can cause you to lose your footing. It seems like each year the area claims another fisherman or two who failed to take proper safety precautions.

Access to the river can be gained from Harpers Ferry Road near Sandy Hook on the Maryland shore and also from the town of Harpers Ferry on the West Virginia bank. The wade-fishing is excellent from the Dam #3 remnants downstream to below the US Rt. 340 bridge. But be careful in this water.

Section V. Brunswick, Md., to Seneca, Md.
Back-in Boat Ramps

1. Brunswick ramp, C&O Canal NHP, Town of Brunswick, Md.

2. Point of Rocks ramp, C&O Canal NHP, below Md. Rt. 15 bridge over Potomac.

3. Dickerson ramp, C&O Canal NHP, at mouth of Monocacy River near Dickerson, Md.

4. Nolands Ferry, C&O Canal NHP, Md. Rt. 85, south of Frederick, Md.

5. Edwards Ferry, C&O Canal NHP, Md. Rt. 107 near Poolesville, Md.

6. Seneca ramp, C&O Canal NHP, Reddick Road, south of Poolesville, Md., at mouth of Little Seneca Creek.

Suggested Float Trips

1. Brunswick to Point of Rocks, 6.3 miles
Put-in: Brunswick C&O Canal NHP ramp, Town of Brunswick.
Take-out: Point of Rocks C&O Canal NHP ramp, at Md. Rt. 15 bridge over river.

2. Edwards Ferry to Seneca, 8.7 miles
Put-in: Edwards Ferry C&O Canal NHP ramp, off Offut Road, near Poolesville, Md.
Take-out: Seneca C&O Canal NHP ramp, Reddick Road, south of Poolesville, Md.

In many ways, this might be the best section of the river. The Potomac broadens greatly after the confluence with the Shenandoah, and studies by biologists have shown that the river is much more fertile in terms of aquatic insects.

I haven't floated the river much downstream of Point of Rocks, because the river is generally deep enough to fish with my riverboat. I have floated from Brunswick to Point of Rocks many times, and recommend the trip highly.

All of this section is much the same, with long, fairly deep pools, and short riffles and drops that require some navigation by the boater.

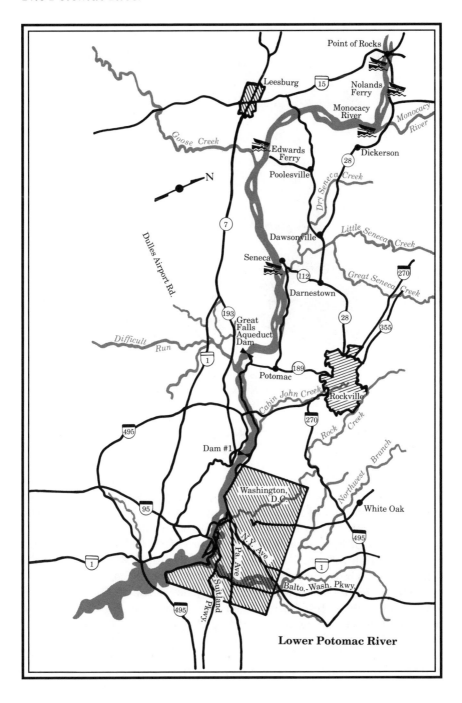

Lower Potomac River

*Lefty Kreh unhooks a big smallmouth taken
from the Seneca section of the Potomac.*

Most of the river from Brunswick down can be navigated by boaters
with a properly rigged boat.

Below Dickerson an interesting situation develops as a result of
the Dickerson power plant and its warm water discharge. The water
being discharged into the river creates a warm water fishery, even during the coldest part of the year. This means that during winter when
the water on the Virginia shore might be below 40 degrees, the Maryland shore will have a water temperature of 48 to 50 degrees, which
means the fish continue to feed actively all winter. Fishing below the
Dickerson discharge is popular all the way down to the Seneca area.

The Potomac is a very diverse fishery, one of the better smallmouth
rivers in this book. In addition, the channel cat fishing is excellent and
very popular with a legion of anglers. The walleyes offer another outstanding fishing opportunity.

Because of its excellent accessibility, the Potomac is one of the
hardest fished of the rivers in this book. But despite the fishing pres-

sure, the river continues to produce outstanding catches of small-mouths. Several anglers that I know of land twenty or more four-pound-plus smallmouths each season.

Much to their credit, many of the better anglers release a majority of the big bass they catch. It's a good thing, because the river's smallmouth fishery would not long withstand the kind of intelligent fishing pressure it is now receiving if all of the big fish caught were ending up in the frying pan.

FOURTEEN

The Susquehanna River

The Susquehanna River is different from the other rivers in this book, and the differences are many and varied. While most of the other rivers begin as mountain brooks, the Susquehanna traces its beginning to a lake—Lake Otsego near Cooperstown, New York.

Starting in New York, the river runs some 444 miles, draining some of the most fertile lands in the East. Near Northumberland, Pennsylvania, the North Branch is joined by the West Branch, and the now-much-larger river continues the trip south through the state, through the sprawling Harrisburg/Middletown metropolis, through four impoundments, to cross the tidal line near Port Deposit, Maryland.

Over the years the river has endured its share of man-made horrors: pollution of various types from the many cities it passes in New York and Pennsylvania, acid from coal mining on the West Branch, and silt, herbicides, and pesticides from farming operations. But the river has bounced back from the abuses and by standard measurements, such as water alkalinity and aquatic insect life, the river may be the most fertile of any in this book.

Those not familiar with the Susquehanna may find it intimidating at first sight. In the section covered in this book, from Northumberland down to Port Deposit, the river is quite broad—nearly a mile in width in some areas. But don't be alarmed by first impressions because, although the river is wide, the current flow at normal water levels is usually moderate, and most of the Susquehanna is really quite tame compared to the real roughnecks—the lower New and the Potomac near Harpers Ferry.

The Susquehanna is an outstanding fishery. With all its surface acres of water, with the excellent forage base of aquatic insects and baitfish, and with all the perfect habitat formed by countless rocks, rock formations, islands, and weed beds, the river is the perfect nursery for smallmouth bass, channel catfish, walleyes, and a variety of panfish.

108

The Susquehanna is also basically a shallow river—so shallow, in fact, that I don't consider it good float-fishing water. Larry Jackson, the Pennsylvania Game Commission biologist in charge of the section from Northumberland downstream to Middletown, agreed. "The river is so spread out, with few defined channels, that float fishermen can find themselves grounded if they choose the wrong side of an island to follow down," Larry said.

For this reason we will concentrate on the usual method of fishing the river: launching a small, shallow-draft riverboat from one of the Fish Commission access sites, and fishing the area near the site. The other popular method is to wade-fish the river. The Susquehanna is a great wade-fishing river.

GAMEFISH OF THE SUSQUEHANNA

Smallmouth Bass

The regulars on the Susquehanna feel they fish the best smallmouth river in the country. That's a big statement, and my research—in the form of fishing the river many times (certainly not scientific, but highly entertaining)—shows that this water does support an incredible number of smallmouths.

The rolling waters below Conowingo Dam offer excellent habitat for many species of gamefish.

It should be pointed out that the river does not have the documented track record of producing big smallmouths that some of the other rivers have. The James in Virginia and the New in Virginia and West Virginia both produce far more trophy fish in terms of angler citations. But it is possible that Pennsylvania anglers don't bother with registering their fish for citations, so this means of measurement could hardly be considered definitive. But without the citations it is hard to document the river as a regular producer of trophy-sized smallmouth bass.

The river does receive heavy fishing pressure. In fact, I think the Harrisburg/Middletown section of the river receives more hard fishing than any section of any river I have fished. This could lead to a large number of bass being cropped off before reaching trophy size, with the resulting lack of citation fish to be registered with the Fish Commission.

On the other hand, I have never fished a river with better concentrations of smallmouths, and have never caught fish in better shape. The fertile river grows bass that are plump and sassy and, during the fall, when the fish are really on the feed, the average size per fish is the best I've ever experienced.

A further interesting observation on the Susquehanna smallmouths is that the fish seem to be quite attuned to feeding on aquatic insects, which, of course, is simply their adapting to available forage. The river is extremely rich in insect life and the fish are responding to the opportunity.

Bob Clouser, a good friend and the owner of a fly-fishing shop and guiding business in the Middletown area, has spent years observing the bass and has developed several flies to take advantage of the insect diet of the river smallmouths. Even the larger bass on this river enjoy feeding on the prolific hatches of mayflies and caddis flies.

A further interesting note is that the river has a terrific crayfish population. This is probably the result of the limestone-influenced water. At any rate, crayfish are a staple of the Susquehanna bass, and lures and flies (such as the Clouser Crayfish) that imitate crayfish are very effective.

This is one of the few rivers where I noticed anglers regularly fishing live crayfish as bait.

Largemouth Bass
Studies by biologist Larry Jackson and interviews with anglers indicate that largemouths aren't very frequently encountered in the Sus-

Bob Clouser of Harrisburg with a small fish taken on fly rod tackle. The area near Three Mile Island (in background) *is top smallmouth habitat.*

quehanna. There are some largemouths in the slower-moving pools and occasionally some big largemouths are caught, but for the most part this is not a fish you are likely to catch.

Walleye
The Fish Commission has an ongoing walleye-stocking program in the river to supplement natural reproduction, which has been less than satisfactory. The fish are found throughout the section, but are concentrated in certain spots at certain times of the year. The waters below several dams—Dock Street, York Haven, and Red Hill—are noted walleye areas, and Larry Jackson said that, in the fall and winter, fish in the twenty-inch class are regularly taken from below the dams by walleye specialists.

Muskie
Like the walleye, the muskie fishery in the Susquehanna is maintained by a stocking program, so the river supports an excellent population of

trophy muskie. Fish weighing thirty pounds and more are taken each season. As is the case in all the rivers, the muskie are usually found in the deeper pools, frequently near the mouth of tributary streams, of which the river has many.

The Susquehanna has an impressive forage base for the muskie, mostly suckers and small carp. There are few pools long enough for serious trolling in this river, so the preferred method is casting large plugs. The area just below and above the U.S. Route 76 (the Pennsylvania Turnpike) bridge features some deep pools that have produced a number of trophy muskie over the years.

Channel Catfish

As would be expected of such a fertile river, the Susquehanna is an excellent channel cat fishery. The fish are distributed throughout the river, but concentrations can be found below dams such as Dock Street, York Haven, and Conowingo.

The waters below Conowingo offer catfish action as good as it gets anywhere. The waters are full of ground-up fish that have been processed through the turbines, and the result is a catfish buffet that draws the fish like a magnet. You can fish the dam from the fishermen's catwalk, or launch a boat. This is big water with a heavy current during peak generating output, so boaters must be careful.

Carp

Carp are adaptable creatures, and flourish under the worst of conditions. In a river like the Susquehanna, they do extremely well. The fish are found throughout the sections in this book and grow quite large in the river. Fish weighing over twenty pounds aren't uncommon, and if you want to hook a brute, try the pools below Conowingo during minimum flow release—the fish are concentrated at this time. And some of the pools will be full of carp in the twenty-pound-plus class.

Panfish

The Susquehanna has an excellent rock bass population, and many fishermen seem to fish for them specifically and enjoy catching them. This cropping by fishermen may be one reason that the rock bass you catch are usually in excellent shape, with a nice average size. An excellent forage base also has a lot to do with it.

Other panfish include the sunfishes—the red breast, longear, pumpkinseed, and bluegill—and in certain areas crappies are found.

A mixed bag of cats and a striper from earlier days below Conowingo.

Susquehanna anglers like their panfish fishing, and the little fish are an important part of the overall fishing opportunity provided by the river.

ACCESS TO THE RIVER

Access to the river is very good. In fact, many of the river regulars complain that the access is too good. Because of the nature of the river, with its low water levels during most of the summer months, many access points are needed. For example, the only public ramp below the the Dock Street dam in Harrisburg is all the way down at Middletown. This is a run of about four miles, and a distance that will take quite some time to cover during the low water levels of late summer and early fall.

Since nearly all of the land along the Susquehanna is privately owned, there are also a number of private ramps along the river, and in some cases you can launch there for a small fee. But as has been the policy for all the rivers, the ramps we will look at are the publicly owned ramps, with free access and adequate parking.

Selected Sections of the River

Section I. Sunbury, Pa., to Falmouth, Pa.
Back-in Ramps

1. Shamokin Dam access: 8th Street, off US Rt. 11/15.

2. Hoover Island access: 3½ miles south of Selinsgrove on US Rt. 11/15.

3. McKee Half Falls access: off US Rt. 11/15, south of McKee Half Falls.

4. Swaggert Island access: 3 miles north of Liverpool on US Rt. 11/15.

5. Millersburg access: Pa. Rt. 147, west end of Moore Street.

6. Montgomery Ferry access: Village of Montgomery Ferry, off US Rt. 11/15.

7. Halifax access: Pa. Rt. 147, south of Halifax.

8. New Buffalo access: 1.3 miles north of New Buffalo, on US Rt. 11/15.

9. Fort Hunter access: US Rt. 22/322, .6 miles north of Rockville bridge.

10. West Fairview access: off US Rt. 11, at Conodoquinet Creek, south of Enola.

11. City Island access: Harrisburg, US Rt. 22/322 on east side of river or US Rt. 11/15 on west side of river to Walnut and Market streets.

12. Middletown access: Pa. Rt. 441 to South Union Street, at mouth of Swatara Creek.

13. Goldsboro access: This is a deepwater impounded access area, behind the York Haven dam, east side of Goldsboro.

14. Falmouth access: one mile below York Haven dam off Pa. Rt. 441.

This section of the Susquehanna is basically similar to the others in that the river is a wide, slow-moving waterway, liberally dotted with

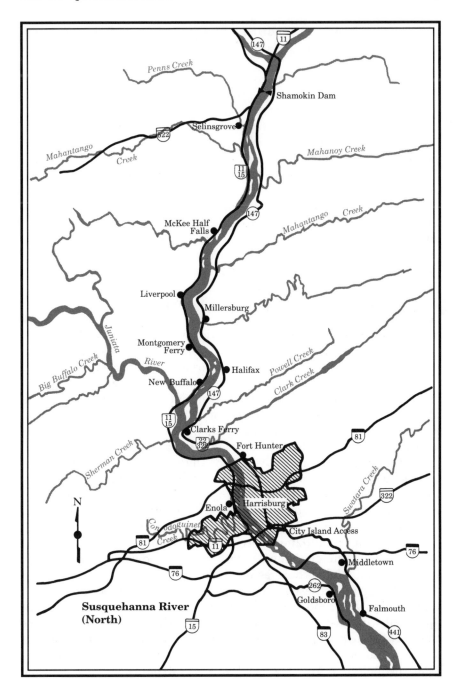

Shamokin Dam

Selinsgrove

Mahanoy Creek

McKee Half Falls

Mahantango Creek

Liverpool

Millersburg

Montgomery Ferry

Halifax

Powell Creek

New Buffalo

Clark Creek

Clarks Ferry

Fort Hunter

Big Buffalo Creek

Juniata River

Sherman Creek

N

Enola

Harrisburg

Conodoguinet Creek

Swatara Creek

City Island Access

Middletown

Susquehanna River (North)

Goldsboro

Falmouth

Penns Creek

Mahantango Creek

islands (both large and small) and numerous rock and grass outcroppings that look like islands but are really small breaks in shallow water.

The area I'm most familiar with is the stretch from the Dock Street dam in Harrisburg downstream to the York Haven dam at Three Mile Island. Most of the other water looks very much the same.

The one feature that distinguishes the Susquehanna from the others in this book is that it is rather shallow throughout, with the occasional deep pool. This makes for a very nice body of water in which to fish from a small, shallow-draft boat, or by wading during the summer and early fall.

As one can ascertain from the maps, several roads generally follow the river. From the west side above Harrisburg, U.S. Route 11/15 allows the fisherman to travel alongside the river and pick out spots to enter the water either by boat or by wading.

South of Harrisburg, and on the east side of the river, Pa. Route 441 gives the angler good access to the water.

One aspect of this section that is quite important are the two areas below dams that attract a lot of attention from fishermen. The Dock Street dam in Harrisburg is very popular with smallmouth fishermen, particularly in the spring. The tendency of the bigger bass to bunch up in this area during the prespawning period was reportedly one of the reasons that more restrictive regulations were requested by fishermen.

The tailrace area below York Haven dam is another very significant fishery, and rated by many as one of the most productive walleye and channel catfish areas in this section. Excellent access to this area is available from the Fish Commission ramp at Falmouth.

Another area where I have personally enjoyed excellent fishing is the section of river from Marysville upstream to the confluence with the Juniata near Amity Hall. Much of this section is quite shallow and makes for excellent wading during the summertime. The waters hold an abundance of aquatic insect life, and during the summer months this makes for outstanding fly-rodding with small surface poppers or even dry flies. The smallmouth bass in the Susquehanna seem to be very insect-minded in their feeding habits.

Although all of these rivers contain a good forage base of insects (or they wouldn't be good smallmouth rivers), an informal, nonscientific appraisal while fishing indicates to me that the Susquehanna may be the most fertile and productive of them all. Despite the many problems that have faced the river over the years, it remains quite fertile and relatively pollution free. The result is a very dynamic warm water fishery with an excellent aquatic insect and crustacean (crayfish) forage base. As a result the smallmouth bass, panfish, and other gamefish show impressive growth rates.

Section II. Holtwood Dam, Pa., to Port Deposit, Md.
Back-in Boat Ramps

1. Muddy Creek access: Pa. Rt. 74 south from Red Lion, turn east (left) on Pa. Rt. 372. At the west end of Norman Wood Bridge turn south (right) on Slab-Holtwood road, and go approximately 1.5 miles to launching facilities. This access is a cooperative effort between the Pennsylvania Fish Commission and the Philadelphia Electric Company.

2. Lapidum access: Md. Rt. 161 south of Darlington to Stafford Road. Cross Deer Creek and follow road through Susquehanna State Park to boat ramp site near Lapidum.

The section could also be called the upper and lower ends of Conowingo Reservoir. This is a very important section for two reasons: The areas are productive fisheries, and the excellent access makes them very popular with fishermen from population centers such as York and Baltimore.

The upper end of Conowingo Pond (called Conowingo Reservoir in Maryland) is an outstanding smallmouth fishery, and quite unusual in many respects. Above the access ramp at the mouth of Muddy Creek, the river is divided into many channels that wind their way through a maze of small islands and rock formations. The area above the ramp features several big islands, such as Upper Bear Island and Lower Bear Island, as well as Piney Island, just above the Pa. Rt. 372 bridge. The loose rocks have formed some interesting crannies, and small pockets have been worn into solid rock by the moving waters. Some of these pockets are much deeper than you would expect, and by casting small lures into them you can often pick up nice smallmouths. The best lure for this pocket fishing is usually a jig of some type.

Smallmouth bass are the principal gamefish above Muddy Creek, but the area also produces panfish, catfish, and occasionally something exotic like a muskie or a white perch/striped bass hybrid.

The area below Conowingo Dam was once the glamour spot of freshwater fishing in Maryland. The area offered excellent numbers of migrating American and hickory shad in the springtime as well as

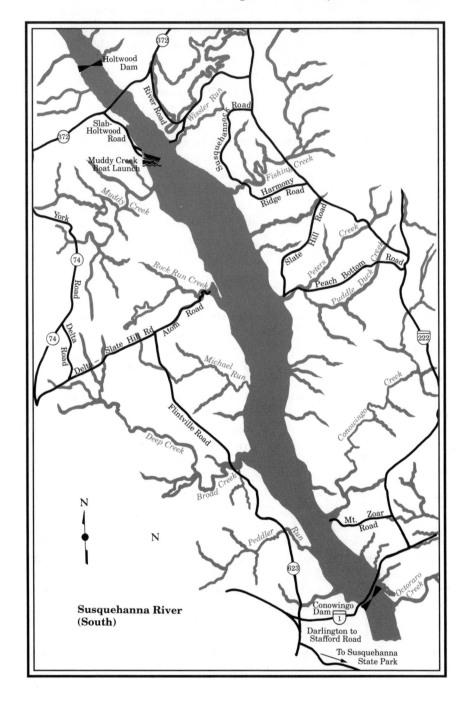

Susquehanna River (South)

stripers that moved into the river to feed on the gizzard shad and other forage fish being passed through the turbines during generating periods. In addition, there were smallmouth bass, catfish, carp, and other species such as muskie and walleye that were assumed to be escapees from the stocking programs being carried out in Conowingo Reservoir.

But the shad and the stripers fared poorly during the 1980s and eventually Maryland was forced to forbid fishing for stripers and migrating shad in an attempt to preserve the remaining fish as brood stock for the future.

With the ban on striper and shad fishing, the waters below the Conowingo Dam became a catfish, carp, and, to a lesser degree, smallmouth bass fishery. This is the official line. Another type of fishing that became popular with some anglers was a catch-and-release striper fishery. With the ban on sport and commercial fishing, stripers began to repopulate the area in good numbers. The area began to attract fishermen out to catch stripers under the pretense of fishing for something else.

This is a difficult violation to prosecute because it is almost impossible to prove that anglers who say they are after, say, smallmouth

Lefty Kreh and Captain Earl Ashenfelter with a nice striper taken on fly rod tackle before the ban on striper fishing was enacted.

bass, are really trying to catch stripers. The result of this unsportsman-like behavior is stripers being caught again and again. Studies are showing some very significant losses—fish that are dying from the stress of being caught and handled by fishermen.

As far as I'm concerned, this premeditated effort to catch striped bass is unconscionable behavior. The striper is a gamefish in deep trouble. Spawning success for the striped bass, as a result of pollution of the Chesapeake Bay and some of its major tributaries, has been terrible for more than a decade. This trend seems to be reversing as efforts are underway to improve the water quality. But in the meantime, the remaining fish must be protected to insure a viable brood stock when the habitat has been improved.

Fisherman after other species will catch the occasional striper. I've done so myself while fishing for smallmouth bass in the area. But to go after stripers specifically, with lures more likely to catch stripers than other fish, is an incredibly blatant violation of the spirit of the law. The striped bass needs the help of anglers if it is ever to return to the list of available gamefish. Please help by leaving the remaining fish alone as much as possible.

The area below the dam should be an excellent smallmouth bass fishery, but has never seemed to meet expectations. Finally a study of the area by Maryland fisheries biologists identified the problem.

Smallmouth bass were tagged and recaptured, and the studies showed that, while smallmouth were in the area below the dam during spring, the fish would move out when summer approached. They were moving farther downstream because the high summertime water temperatures and low levels of dissolved oxygen were unsuitable conditions during periods of limited water releases at the dam.

Other species, such as catfish and carp, which are more tolerant of higher water temperatures and low oxygen levels, remained in the pools below the dam, but the smallmouths would move out, and only return to feed on gizzard shad during generating periods, when the oxygen level would increase.

The studies also showed a very poor aquatic insect population—another result of the low oxygen levels and high temperatures during the summer months.

Help may be on the way for the bass, however, because in 1988 the Philadelphia Electric Company (PECO), the Maryland Department of Natural Resources, and the Pennsylvania Fish Commission signed an agreement that includes a minimum year-round flow rate below the dam, and measures to increase the oxygen level through oxygen injec-

Captain Ashenfelter with a big cat from below Conowingo Dam.

tion or intake aeration, or by spilling water from the upper levels of the reservoir through spill gates.

Another important part of the agreement concerns the migrating shad. The power company is to build a fish lift on the east side of the powerhouse that will have a capacity of 1.5 million shad; and once that lift reaches capacity, another is to be built on the west side of the powerhouse. The goal is to eliminate the dam as a blockage to migrating fish.

Despite the problems with water temperatures and oxygen levels, the area below the dam has remained an excellent channel catfish spot. The river offers exceptional catfish habitat, particularly when water is released during generating periods—the high volume of food processed through the turbines attracts the cats like a magnet.

There are several ways of fishing the area. The power company has a fishermen's catwalk on the face of the dam that allows you to fish straight down into the churning waters below. This is one of the more interesting fishing opportunities you will find on the rivers. The technique is to use enough weight on the line to keep the bait down near the bottom where the catfish will be feeding. The preferred bait is usually shrimp, or a piece of fish of some type.

One problem is getting a heavy fish up from the water after it is hooked. The regulars on the catwalk have developed a system of using a basket type of net that they can lower by rope and maneuver beneath a hooked fish. Without the net, many fish would be lost.

You can also fish this area by boat. The public ramp at Lapidum offers good access, and during moderate releases you can maneuver your riverboat upstream toward the dam area.

Boaters should note that during minimum water releases from the dam the water will be quite shallow and running the river can be a problem. When the release is increased, the boating situation is improved, but then you are dealing with some formidable current.

When you hear the siren from the dam signifying an upcoming release, you should be prepared for a rapid increase in both water level and flow rate. If you are anchored, this means you'd better be able to retrieve your anchor or have a sharp knife ready to cut the rope. Boaters have drowned here when their boat was pulled under—the waters quickly rose and they were unable to get the anchor up.

During maximum generating periods, this is a big, brawling river with extremely strong currents—no place for dinky little boats or balky outboards. If you are properly equipped, the fishing can be excellent during generating periods, but make no mistake about the fact that this river can be deadly for those who fail to show proper respect for the high water and heavy currents that occur periodically.

FIFTEEN

The Juniata River

The Juniata is a special little river. Although it is one of the smaller rivers in the book, it is also in many ways one of the best. The Juniata offers everything an angler could want: good fishing for a variety of gamefish, excellent access, and, best of all, a gently moving waterway, without major rapids or dams—a river that at normal flow levels is safe to boat or wade if normal precautions are taken.

The river has two branches that meet near Lewistown. Each branch is an excellent fishery in its own right. The Raystown Branch, which is the stream impounded to form Raystown Lake, is a significant tributary.

The section we will cover is the main stem of the river, beginning at Lewistown, downstream to the confluence with the Susquehanna at Amity Hall.

Before moving on, it should be noted that the tailrace area below Raystown Dam is an area that anglers should consider. Not only are smallmouth bass, catfish, and walleye found there, but also striped bass and very big brown trout. The stripers and trout are thought to be escapees from the lake. This is a developing story as more stripers and trophy brown trout are caught each year, and is certainly something for the angler to keep in mind when planning a Juniata River trip.

GAMEFISH OF THE JUNIATA

Smallmouth Bass
The Juniata is an excellent smallmouth river. Larry Jackson, the Pennsylvania Fish Commission biologist in charge of it, noted that the river is extremely fertile. It drains an area rich in limestone, and the alkaline waters create an environment ideal for many species of aquatic insects, and, in turn, baitfish and gamefish.

The Juniata is productive both in terms of quality and quantity. The average weekend float fisherman can expect to land plenty of small and scrappy smallmouths and the occasional trophy bass. The largest I found when reviewing citation records weighed six pounds, eight ounces, which is a very big smallmouth from any river, particularly so from one of the smaller rivers in the book.

Many of the Juniata fishermen prefer live bait for smallmouths and the hellgramite is one of the better baits for those, as well as for panfish and channel catfish. Minnows and stone cats (madtoms) are also popular live baits.

Fly-fishing for smallmouths is also popular and, with the many mayfly and caddis fly hatches on the river during the summer months, can be quite productive.

Largemouth Bass

Unlike many of the rivers, the Juniata is not a noted largemouth fishery. Larry Jackson said that his studies of the river have shown few largemouth bass, and reports from fishermen indicate the same. As Jackson noted, there will always be the odd fish that escaped from a pond or lake environment and set up housekeeping in the river, but largemouths are not one of the more likely catches here.

Channel Catfish

Channel cats are found throughout most of the area that we're looking at, and are a popular gamefish with certain anglers. This river is somewhat unusual in that it doesn't have places such as tailrace areas below dams to concentrate the fish, but pools below riffles and behind rock ledge formations often hold good numbers of channel cats.

Walleye

Walleyes are one of the featured attractions on the river. The Fish Commission has supplemented natural reproduction with yearly and every-other-year stockings for more than a decade, and combination stringers of bass and walleyes are one of the reasons many anglers find this river so appealing. Larry Jackson noted that the walleyes are found throughout the area, and said that the walleyes will usually be found in the longer, deeper pools behind large rocks and ledges. "I euphemistically call them 'walleye pools,'" Larry said. "The walleye fisherman recognizes them—the bigger pools, with slower-moving water, that might not be the ideal place for smallmouths, but where you would expect to find walleyes or maybe a muskie."

Some of the Juniata walleyes grow quite large, and Jackson said that a ten-pound walleye would not be unusual, but the average fish are more in the fifteen- to twenty-inch range.

Muskie

Muskies are never what you would call plentiful, and this is the case on the Juniata. The river is, however, one of the better muskie rivers in the book, and regularly produces fish in the twenty-five- to thirty-pound class. Larry Jackson of the Pennsylvania Fish Commission describes both the Juniata and the Susquehanna as "trophy fisheries" for muskies, and that's an apt description.

Muskies are loners and are usually found in the slower-moving, deeper pools. However, in the springtime one of the more popular local techniques is what the regulars call creek-hopping. The Juniata has many tributaries, and in the spring suckers ascend them to spawn. The muskie hunters will drive from creek mouth to creek mouth, and cast spoons and large lures near the confluence of the creeks and the river in hopes of catching a muskie feeding on the suckers. It's one of the more productive techniques, I'm told.

Panfish

The Juniata is an excellent panfish stream. Rock bass are the primary panfish species, followed by redbreast sunfish. Rock bass are the more plentiful, however, and I get the distinct impression that Pennsylvania anglers enjoy and appreciate rock bass more than anglers from the other states. This is just a feeling, based upon talking with anglers on all of the rivers, but a significant number on the Juniata said they were fishing for rock bass specifically, and enjoyed catching them.

The rock bass are found in the same areas as the smallmouth and are caught on basically the same baits, lures, and flies. The fertile nature of the river makes it possible for the fish to grow to nice size, and pan-sized rock bass are caught on nearly every trip when the angler is using baits and lures for smallmouths.

ACCESS TO THE RIVER

Access to the Juniata is excellent. U.S. Rt. 22/322 parallels the river for most of the section, and there are nine Fish Commission landings in this area. The Juniata is an excellent float-fishing river, but is also ideally suited to wading.

In some areas, you might have to cross private land when attempting to reach the river at spots other than the Fish Commission areas. Keep in mind that permission is required of the landowner in such cases. However, the access from Commission facilities is more than adequate if you have problems obtaining permission to cross privately owned property.

Suggested Float Trips—The following float trips begin and end at Fish Commission access areas on the river. Each Commission area features a back-in boat ramp that is also suitable for small trailered riverboats. Most of the areas will be difficult to run during the summer months; but they can usually be navigated, although you may have to get out and pull through certain spots.

1. Point Access to Newton Hamilton, approximately 15 miles
   Put-in: Point Access, Pennsylvania Fish Commission (PFC) access area, located off US Rt. 22, north of Mt. Union.
   Take-out: Newton Hamilton, PFC access area, located in Newton Hamilton, on Pa. Rt. 986.

2. Newton Hamilton to Granville, approximately 18 miles
   Put-in: Newton Hamilton (described above).
   Take-out: Granville PFC access area, located 3 miles west of Lewistown, off Pa. Rt. 103. Follow signs.

3. Granville to Mifflintown, approximately 20 miles
   Put-in: Granville (described above).
   Take-out: Mifflintown PFC access area, located .5 mile west of Mifflintown on Pa. Rt. 32 (old US Rt. 22).

4. Mifflintown to Walker, approximately 6 miles
   Put-in: Mifflintown (described above).
   Take-out: Walker PFC access area, located in village of Mexico, Pa. Rt. 32 (old US Rt. 22).

5. Walker to Muskrat Springs, approximately 5 miles
   Put-in: Walker (described above).
   Take-out: Muskrat Springs PFC access area, located at village of Center, 2.5 miles east of Mexico, on Pa. Rt. 32 (old US Rt. 22).

6. Muskrat Springs to Thompsontown, approximately 6 miles
   Put-in: Muskrat Springs (described above).
   Take-out: Thompsontown PFC access area, located .5 mile south of Thompsontown on Pa. Rt. 333.

7. Thompsontown to Greenwood, approximately 8 miles
   Put-in: Thompsontown (described above).
   Take-out: Greenwood PFC access area, 2.5 miles south of Millerstown, off US Rt. 22/322 on Pa. Rt. 32 (old US Rt. 22).

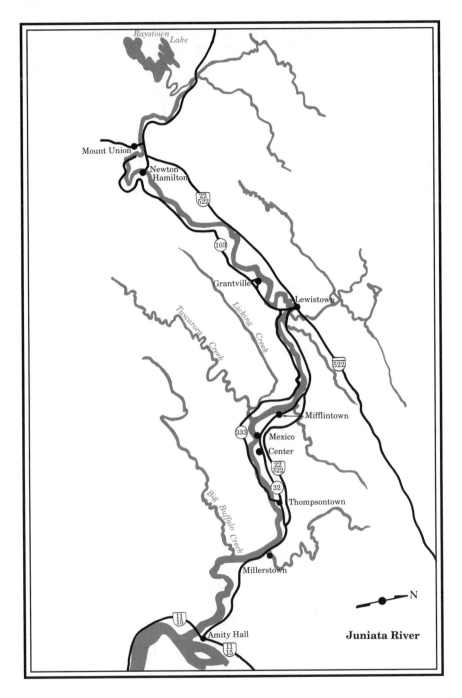

Raystown Lake

Mount Union

Newton
Hamilton

22
522

103

Grantville

Licking Creek

Tuscarora Creek

Lewistown

522

Mifflintown

333

Mexico
Center

22
322

32

Thompsontown

Big Buffalo Creek

Millerstown

N

11
15

Amity Hall

11
15

Juniata River

8. Greenwood to Amity Hall, approximately 12 miles
Put-in: Greenwood (described above).
Take-out: Amity Hall PFC access area, in the village of Amity
Hall, off US Rt. 11/15.

As you can see, the float trip possibilities on the river are quite
varied. Many are very long floats, and are usually broken up into two-
day camping trips. The shorter floats are perfect one-day outings, and
my favorite is the Thompsontown–to–Greenwood run.

During the spring and again in the fall, when the river is up a bit,
you can fish most of the areas by launching your riverboat and motor-
ing from spot to spot. This is the best bet for muskie and walleye fishing, when you might want to fish a particular hole or pool thoroughly.

The river is also excellent for wading, and during the summer
months this is perhaps the most popular method of fishing the waters.
The Juniata is a relatively gentle river to wade as compared to, say, the
New, and waders can fish most of the water safely if normal precautions are taken.

Despite the easy access to the river, the Juniata isn't as heavily
fished as you might expect. The Susquehanna receives far more fishing
pressure, and many of the better fishermen concentrate on the bigger
river because they feel a little river like the Juniata might not hold
trophy fish.

But the records don't support this theory, and although many of the
Juniata regulars may not appreciate my bringing their river this attention, I feel that, acre for acre, the Juniata is a better fishery than its big
sister, the Susquehanna.

SIXTEEN

The James River

Fishermen and outdoors writers from the mid-Atlantic region often engage in interesting arguments on the merits of the various rivers in the region, and almost everyone has an opinion on which offers the best fishing opportunities.

The James will have many supporters, and not without cause—it has everything a great river should: excellent water quality, a superb forage base to support its gamefish populations, and adequate access for fishermen who wish to test the waters.

In terms of productivity, the James is unrivaled as a smallmouth river. When I scanned the Virginia Commission of Game and Inland Fisheries records of citation smallmouth bass and muskies for over a ten-year period, it became clear that the James is in a class by itself as a smallmouth river, typically producing more than three times as many citation smallmouths as its closest rival, the New River in Virginia.

The James has both the size and the length to produce big fish. Starting near Eagle Rock, and traveling downstream to Richmond, the angler has approximately 200 miles of prime fishing waters. Along the way, the river displays many changes as it heads out of the mountains and enters the piedmont region on the way to becoming a huge tidal river below Richmond.

There are some other interesting facets of this grand old river. For example, geologists tell us that the James is one of the the longest rivers contained completely within the boundaries of one state—Virginia. Beginning in the mountains near the West Virginia border, the James is formed by the confluence of the Cow Pasture and Jackson rivers in Botetourt County and flows through scenic gorges in the Blue Ridge Mountains. Along its course, it drains some of the most fertile land in the mid-Atlantic.

GAMEFISH OF THE JAMES

Smallmouth Bass

The James is arguably the best smallmouth river in the region, as measured both in terms of numbers of fish and in terms of trophy fish. The number of citation fish (those weighing over four pounds) that the river produces is nothing short of amazing. Beginning in 1985 the river has produced over 300 citation smallmouth per season—nearly three times as many as the New.

The river has all the necessary ingredients to produce big smallmouths. While visiting the river I have taken the time to conduct a few surveys of the aquatic insects and forage fish in the river and, although admittedly unscientific in my approach, I have been able to see that the river offers a nice selection of mayflies, caddis flies, and stone flies. I've also noted excellent fly hatches during summer evenings. Both mayflies of several species and caddis flies are quite evident. Several of the mayflies present are nontolerant of pollution, indicating good water quality. Also very much in evidence are crayfish, which are a staple of the river smallmouth diet.

Outdoors writer Bill Cochran with 4½-pound smallmouth. Photo courtesy Bill Cochran

Stonecats are quite common on the river, and a few of the big fish experts rely on them above all other baits. Most of the experts I've met are live bait fishermen, and during the summer months the stonecat ranks as the top producer of big smallmouths. But big chubs will also work well; and from observations it appears that the James is blessed with a more than adequate base of many forage minnow species.

Largemouth Bass

The upper section of the James—above Lynchburg—is not typical largemouth habitat, although fishermen do report catching a few green bass. The section from Scottsville downstream to the Hardware River is different habitat, with slower waters and channels that weave around islands, and I have taken a few largemouths from this section. One angler had a four-pound largemouth he had taken while casting large plugs for muskie.

Catfish

The James is a good channel catfish river throughout the sections covered in this chapter. The channel cat appears to be quite popular with local anglers because you often see lots of fishermen in boats and on the banks soaking chicken livers or cut bait for the catfish.

Carp

Carp are survivors and they are, of course, found in the James. During my relatively few trips on the James I didn't see many anglers fishing specifically for carp, but during the spring I did see a large number of fish cavorting in the shallows doing their mating dance. An interesting note is that, while I didn't notice many anglers after carp with rod and reel, I did see several people going after the fish with bow and arrow— apparently bow-fishing is quite popular with the James River crew— and they had several very large specimens weighing over twenty pounds each in their boat.

As a sidebar, the bow-fishermen also had a gar they had taken with the bow. (The gar is a disgusting fish, in my opinion, and hardly welcome in a prime smallmouth river like the James.) The archers indicated that gar were not unusual on the upper river, and one can only hope that the fish do not become too firmly established.

Panfish

The redbreast sunfish is quite common along the James and seems to be a fish that anglers specifically go for. Also found in good numbers are rock bass and the occasional bluegill.

While fishing some islands near Scottsville a friend and I ran into a school of large crappies, but talks with locals and fisheries biologists indicate that this might have been a chance encounter since crappies aren't very common on the nontidal section of the James.

Muskie

Muskies are a big-time opportunity in the James. The fish are found primarily in the upper section from Eagle Rock downstream to Glasgow. The hub of the James River muskie fishing activity seem to be in the Springwood area.

Citation records from Virginia show that the James and the New run neck and neck in producing the most trophy muskies. The upper section of the New from Eagle Rock downstream to the Interstate Route 81 bridge is generally characterized by long pools separated by riffles or fish pots. The muskies seem to prefer the deeper waters in the pools and generally hold around an underwater structure, such as a downed tree or a rock formation.

Big muskie from the Springwood section of the James. Photo courtesy Bill Cochran

On the New River, many of the regulars like to troll the long pools, but most of the James River specialists seem to be casters, flinging large lures and retrieving them past likely muskie lairs.

The state has a muskie fishing club called the Old Dominion Musky Hunters and the members of this club typically catch over 50 percent of the state's citation fish in a given year. The muskie fishermen are specialists, and often spend days on the water without a strike, only to hook two or three fish on a day when the conditions are ideal.

But not every fish falls to a specialist. Stories circulate about intrepid float fishermen who hook a monster muskie while fishing for bass or panfish. Most of the toothy predators escape, but sometimes the gods smile on the angler and forty-eight inches of muskie are wrestled to shore or into a canoe, leaving the angler with a story that never dims in the memory.

ACCESS TO THE RIVER

Public access to the James is good. The Commission of Game and Inland Fisheries offers a number of public access points, and private companies, like the Owens-Illinois Corporation, offer access to the river in the Eagle Rock area. At one time, the corporation charged a small fee for this access, but recent information indicates this fee may have been dropped. Boaters will have to check for the latest policy on access to corporate lands.

Selected Sections of the River

Section I. Eagle Rock to Glasgow
Suggested Float Trips

1. Eagle Rock to Springwood, approximately 12 miles
   Put-in: Owens-Illinois Corporation lands, ½ mile upstream of Town of Eagle Rock.
   Take-out: Carry-out access area beneath Va. Rt. 630 bridge in Springwood.

2. Springwood to Buchanan Landing, approximately 5 miles
   Put-in: Springwood access (described above).
   Take-out: Buchanan access, Exchange Street, off US Rt. 11. Concrete ramp suitable for small trailered boats.

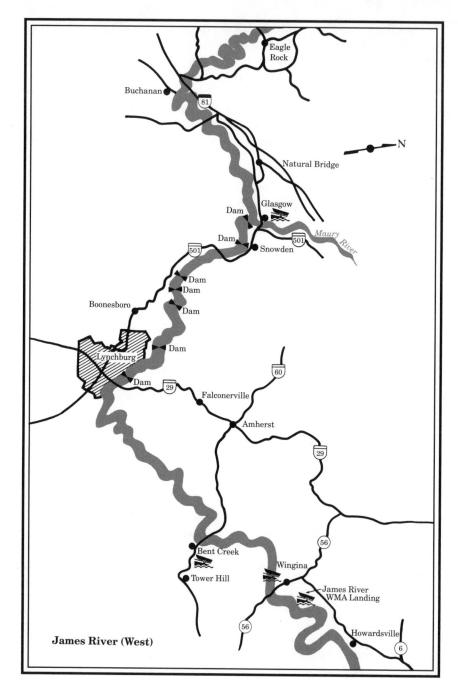

James River (West)

3. Buchanan to Glasgow, approximately 11 miles
Put-in: Buchanan ramp (described above).
Take-out: Glasgow access ramp, off Va. Rt. 684, town of Glasgow.

This section of the James is my favorite. For the most part, the river is relatively narrow and you are treated to views of the mountains for most of the trip.

With a properly rigged riverboat, you can fish much of this water after launching from a ramp. I have taken off from the relatively new Buchanan ramp and motored several miles upstream and downstream with the water level up slightly in the fall. Most of the section is characterized by long pools separated by riffles and ledges. With the right boat, this section of the river can be navigated.

Another ramp that I have used is the new one at Horseshoe Bend, approximately six miles northwest of Buchanan off Va. Rt. 43. This is a nice concrete ramp, but boating is difficult when the river is low. We used it during the fall with the river up slightly and were able to motor several miles upstream toward Eagle Rock.

Another possible float is from Glasgow downstream to Snowden. This is a short float of about five miles, but contains the rather impressive Balcony Falls rapid. This is a serious rapid and for that reason this section is not included in the listing of float trips. Is is a trip for experienced paddlers, and should be a nice ride for veteran canoeists.

Section II. Bent Creek to Goochland
Suggested Float Trips

1. Bent Creek to Wingina, approximately 11 miles
Put-in: Bent Creek landing, off Va. Rt. 26, east on US Rt. 60 from Amherst.
Take-out: Wingina landing, off Va. Rt. 56, west of Wingina.

2. Wingina to Howardsville, approximately 10 miles
Put-in: Wingina landing (described above).
Take-out: Howardsville landing off Va. Rt. 602, northwest of Wingina.

3. Howardsville to Scottsville, approximately 8 miles
Put-in: Howardsville landing (described above).
Take-out: Scottsville landing, off Va. Rt. 20, town of Scottsville.

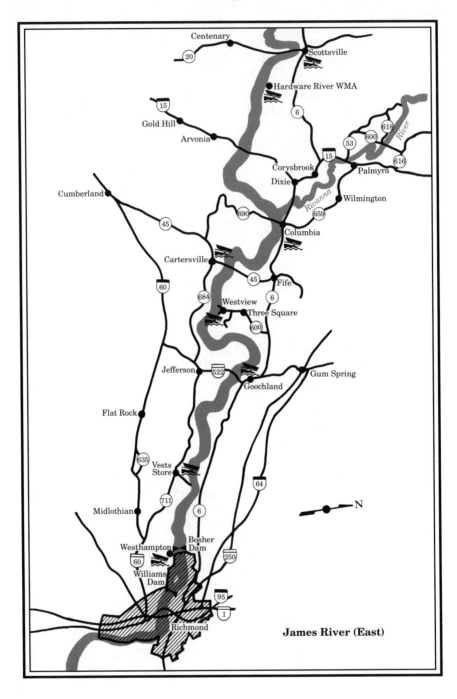

James River (East)

4. Scottsville to Hardware River Wildlife Management Area (WMA), approximately 6 miles
   Put-in: Scottsville landing (described above).
   Take-out: Hardware River WMA, off County Rt. 642.

5. Hardware River WMA to Columbia, approximately 9 miles
   Put-in: Hardware River WMA (described above).
   Take-out: Columbia landing, at County Rt. 690 bridge over river, town of Columbia.

6. Columbia to Cartersville, approximately 7 miles
   Put-in: Columbia landing (described above).
   Take-out: Cartersville landing near Va. Rt. 45 bridge.

7. Cartersville to Westview, approximately 7 miles
   Put-in: Cartersville landing (described above).
   Take-out: Westview landing, off County Rt. 643, near town of Three Square.

8. Westview to Beaumont, approximately 9 miles
   Put-in: Westview landing (described above).
   Take-out: Beaumont landing, US Rt. 522, south of Goochland.

As you can see from the above selection, the float trip possibilities on this part of the James are quite numerous. All the trips on this section are very similar in that the waters are slower-moving than the upper river and the pace of the floating fishermen is quite a lot slower.

Many fishermen combine several of the listed floats into one long trip lasting several days. There are few places in the country better suited for such trips.

For the most part the waters of this section are easily boated by fishermen of moderate boating skill. The exception, of course, would be during periods of high waters after spring or fall rains. You can also successfully boat most of this water with your riverboat. Ramps that I have successfully launched from include the Howardsville landing, the Scottsville landing, and the Columbia landing.

The James is one of our outstanding rivers, perhaps the best of the smallmouth rivers. Although many local anglers complain that the fishing pressure is reaching an unbearable level, my experience has been that the river is still capable of producing a quality outdoor experience with minimum interference from other anglers.

The upper James is typically long pools divided by riffles. Photo courtesy Bill Cochran

The records clearly show that the James is producing many trophy bass and muskie and that it is one of the longest smallmouth fisheries in the country.

When you talk of the complete river fishing experience, the James has it all: beautiful scenery that is determined by your choice of the sections of the river, moderately challenging waters that the average fisherman can safely boat, and a documented history of producing big fish on a regular basis.

What more could the river angler want?

SEVENTEEN

The New River

I must admit to being in awe of the New River. My uncle once lived along its banks in a place that is now underwater as part of Bluestone Lake; and when I was young, he and my father would wow me with stories of giant catfish that they caught on trotlines, of smallmouth bass dying of old age in places that fishermen dared not venture, and of swift, turbulent waters that would claim a life in an instant if the fisherman weren't careful.

The New is an awesome river—at least the section below Bluestone Dam as it gathers momentum for, and passes through, the New River Gorge. But part of the paradox of this body of water is that the gentle little mountain river that flows through Graystone County, Virginia, and into Claytor Lake seems of a different ilk entirely than the brawling, swirling mass of water that rushes through the gorge.

Another situation many of us have a hard time understanding is the name New River, because geologists tell us that it should be called the Old River. Studies of the rocks from the river show that the New is actually the oldest geological feature in North America, predating even the Allegheny Mountains. Some researchers believe that the river is the second oldest in the world, preceded only by the Nile. Archeological studies tell us that there were people living along the river as early as 1300 B.C.

The New is a river shrouded with legends. Early white settlers feared the river and what lay beyond the gorge—a land only the Indians knew. Even the Indians regarded the New with respect, calling it River of Death, in deference to its strong currents and huge waves.

The entire region is a mecca for rock hounds and history buffs. The mountains along the river contain many fossils and interesting rock formations, and the West Virginia section is a memorial to the rise and fall of coal and railroad towns in the region.

One of the most interesting towns on the river is Thurmond. Thurmond is now a busy railroad center, but once enjoyed the reputation of being the "Dodge City of the East," and "Helltown," apparently as a result of its wild atmosphere of gambling, drinking, and other assorted vices.

According to legend, Thurmond was once the site of the longest poker game in history. The game is said to have lasted 14 years, 260 days, nonstop. The old Dun Glen Hotel was the site of this famous game that saw players travel for hundreds of miles to replace those out of money, or stamina, or both.

The New is a superb fishing river—perhaps one of the best in this book. But anglers are warned that many sections of the river are quite dangerous, and they must approach fishing them with the utmost care.

The sections we will be looking at include the upper part in Grayson County, Virginia, above Claytor Lake, where it is a gentle little river with few challenges to the boater.

The area below Claytor Lake, around White Thorn, is much different, but still fishable if the angler is in a decent riverboat and observes proper safety precautions.

The section below Bluestone Lake is a different matter. Just below the Hinton Dam isn't bad, and many fishermen launch small boats here or wade when the water release conditions permit. But the closer you get to the gorge, the rougher the water gets.

The New River Gorge is not for boating fishermen. If you want the ride of your life, through one of the most beautiful areas in North America, then hitch a ride with one of the several whitewater outfitters operating in the gorge. The ride is spectacular, and the big rubber rafts are quite safe. But the heavy water below Prince is not for do-it-yourself types unless they are world class canoeists, or have a death wish.

This is not to say that you can't fish the river below the suggested float trips. There are many places where you can pull the car over and wade or fish from shore. But wading fishermen must also be warned about the heavy currents and uneven river bottom that can make wading tricky. The bottom line? Be very careful in the New below Bluestone Lake.

GAMEFISH OF THE NEW RIVER

Smallmouth Bass
The New is first and foremost a smallmouth river, even though other fish such as muskie, walleye, and catfish are produced in record sizes throughout the river. The smallmouth is undisputed king, and many feel that, overall, in terms of trophy bass potential, the New is the very best in the country.

*Bill Simms, owner of Whitewater Informa-
tion Ltd., with a couple of trophy smallmouths weighing 4½ and 5½ pounds.
Photo courtesy Gerald Almy*

In the Virginia section, the New is a very good smallmouth stream, yet it doesn't rival the James in terms of citation fish produced. The area below Claytor Lake is one of the better-known sections, and trophy smallmouths can be found in the smaller waters above the lake as well.

However, the waters below Bluestone Lake in West Virginia are simply outstanding. This is a large, fertile, smallmouth fishery with all the requirements for growing big fish: food, cover, and very limited fishing pressure because of the very nature of the river. The New dominates the West Virginia citation lists for smallmouth bass, and in a normal year will produce fish weighing up to seven pounds, which for a river smallmouth is simply sensational.

Largemouth Bass
Largemouths are found throughout the New, but the area between Hinton bridge and Sandstone Falls in West Virginia seems to be the most productive largemouth water. The largemouths will usually be found in the deep, slow-moving pools, and fish up to five pounds are taken each season.

Walleye

The New isn't really managed for walleyes in Virginia or West Virginia, but the popular gamefish is present in both states. In Virginia, fish stocked in Claytor Lake have made their way into the upper river, and a few escapees have established viable populations below the lake.

It is much the same in West Virginia. Walleyes have been stocked in Bluestone Reservoir, and, as is always the case, a few fingerling walleye escaped through the dam to take up residence in the river below. The area below Bluestone has what West Virginia biologist Jim Reed called "a small remnant population of walleyes." However, the fish do, well in the fertile river, and walleyes weighing over ten pounds have been taken from the Virginia and West Virginia sections of the New.

Catfish

The New offers perfect habitat for channel catfish and, as might be expected, is a top catfish river. Channel cats are found throughout the river, but as is the case in most rivers with dams, the turbulent waters below the dams are top spots for catfish. This means below Claytor Lake in Virginia, and below Bluestone Lake in West Virginia.

In addition, the river produces flathead catfish—big flathead catfish—weighing up to forty pounds and more.

If you want to concentrate strictly on the big flatheads, use heavy tackle and big bait. A six- to eight-inch chub or a whole fallfish would do nicely.

Muskie

Muskies are found in the New in both Virginia and West Virginia. Virginia manages more intensely for muskies with more stocking, and if the number of citations issued is any indication, the Virginia section of the New is a better muskie stream than the James.

In West Virginia, the muskie stocking program in the New is less emphasized. Some fish do get stocked as fingerlings, but usually only those that are left over from stocking waters more specifically managed for muskie. The fish are there, however, and each year the West Virginia section of the river produces big muskies.

In Virginia the muskie fishing is far more organized, with a dedicated group of specialists who concentrate on the big predators. In West Virginia, most muskie catches seem to be incidental catches by anglers fishing for another species—usually smallmouth bass.

Carp

Carp are found in all sections of the New and, despite the emphasis placed on more glamorous species, visits to the river revealed a number of anglers fishing specifically for carp. The area below the Hinton dam always seems to have a few anglers dipping doughballs for carp.

The New carp grow big; when checking the records, I discovered several years when the New was the top citation carp water in the state.

Panfish

Redbreast sunfish are found throughout the river, as are the ever-popular rock bass. Studies by fisheries biologists have also turned up crappies in some sections, particularly at the upper end of the big lakes.

Hybrid Striped Bass

You don't usually expect to encounter this fish in a smallmouth river like the New. But once again it is a case of the fish escaping through the Bluestone Reservoir dam at Hinton, and doing well after escaping.

This fish is a cross of white bass and striped bass and is a very nice gamefish. Over the past few years, they have been showing up with great regularity below Bluestone, and are being caught on down into the Kanawha River, which is simply the New after it is joined by the Gauley River near Gauley Bridge, West Virginia.

Most hybrids are caught by bass fishermen who are after smallmouth, but angler usually aren't disappointed, because the hybrid is a ferocious fighter—something to do with hybrid vigor, the biologists say.

ACCESS TO THE RIVER

Access to the New is only fair. In Grayson County, Virginia, the Fish and Game Commission has several access sites that provide good opportunities for fishing the waters above Claytor Lake.

Below Claytor Lake is the White Thorn access site, which many fishermen feel is the best in terms of boat-launching facilities and fishing opportunities.

In West Virginia, below Bluestone Lake, the access is good for wading and fishing from shore, but poor for boaters. There aren't any back-in boat ramps, per se, although there are one or two places along River Road heading back toward Sandstone Falls where I have launched my boat. These spots aren't ramps but serve the purpose for a small trailered boat.

There is also carry-in access below Sandstone Falls for canoe and small johnboat anglers, as well as a carry-in access at Meadow Creek that I have used.

In addition, there are countless places on private property where anglers can make their way to the river. Some are rutted, four-wheel-drive trails. You might be able to gain access at such places, but I would be very sure to get permission from the landowner before entering private property. Angry over the condition in which many people leave the areas, with trash scattered and fields rutted by big truck tires, a landowner may decide to take out his frustrations on the next angler caught there. Don't let that be you.

Selected Sections of the River

Section I. Mouth of Wilson to Claytor Lake State Park
Back-in Boat Ramps

1. Fries access: Fish and Game Commission ramp located off Va. Rt. 100, town of Fries.

2. Dublin access: Fish and Game Commission ramp located off Va Rt. 660, 7 miles southeast of Dublin.

3. Claytor Lake State Park ramp, located in the state park, which is south of Dublin on Va. Rt. 660.

Suggested Float Trips

1. Route 21 bridge to Fries access area, approximately 11 miles
   Put-in: Public access area located off US Rt. 21/221, approximately 2 miles north of North Carolina border.
   Take-out: Fries public access area located off Va. Rt. 602, north of Fries.

2. Austinville access to Allisonia, approximately 12 miles
   Put-in: Public access area off Va. Rt. 642 near Austinville.
   Take-out: Public access area off Va. Rt. 693, north of Allisonia.

This section of the upper New River was one of the hardest to research because of the limited formal public access. The land the river flows through is typically rolling farms and wooded ridges. The area is relatively unsettled and access to the river is mostly obtained at bridge crossings.

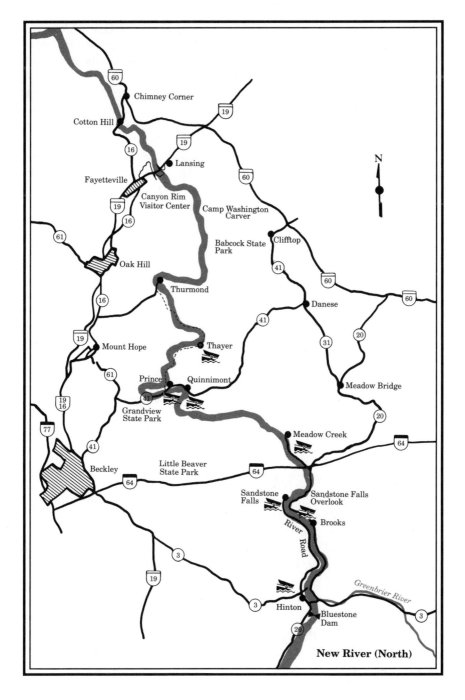

New River (North)

At the time of this writing the Virginia Fish and Game Commission was attempting to provide up to twelve access points on the upper river, by buying and leasing access to privately owned lands and building graveled access points below the bridges.

With only a few exceptions, the upper New is a gentle river that can be handled by average fishermen in canoes and light boats. Higher than normal water levels can quickly change the situation, however, and this section of the river seems to react quickly to periods of rain.

Areas to be very concerned about include the Double Shoals Rapids, which begin about two miles below the low water bridge where Virginia Route 607 crosses the river. This is a Class III or IV series of rapids and is definitely not for the unskilled boater.

Section II. From below Claytor Lake to Bluestone Lake
Back-in Boat Ramps:

1. White Thorn ramp, off Va. Rt. 693, south of Blacksburg.

2. Glen Lyn ramp, located at the US Rt. 460 bridge, approximately 15 miles west of Blacksburg.

3. Narrows ramp, located on the north side of the river, off Va. Rt. 649, in the town of Narrows.

Suggested Float Trips

1. Below Claytor Lake to Radford access, approximately 12 miles
   Put-in: Public access point just below Claytor Lake Dam, off Va. Rt. 605.
   Take-out: Access point off Va. Rt. 114, near town of Radford.

2. Eggleston access point to Pembroke, approximately 7 miles
   Put-in: Eggleston public access, just below County Rt. 730 bridge, town of Eggleston.
   Take-out: Pembroke access point, located off County Rt. 652 at the New River Canoe Livery. (*Note:* This is one of the few times that a private, commercial access point has been recommended, but the small access fee is well spent in this case.)

This section of the New provides excellent opportunities for anglers equipped with good riverboats. One of the most popular sections of the entire river is the White Thorn access area, which features a series of long deep pools that are noted for producing a large number of trophy muskies each season.

The ramps at Glen Lyn and Narrows also offer excellent opportunities to put in and run for short distances with the right river rig.

Areas to watch out for include Big Falls about two miles below McCoy, the Narrows rapids about two miles below the town of Narrows, and Shumate Falls, about eight miles below Narrows. The Narrows rapids is a popular float tube area with the college students from Virginia Tech, located at Blacksburg, but this is not the place for the average fisherman to learn fast water boating techniques.

Section III. Bluestone Lake to Thurmond

Back-in Boat Ramps: None

Suggested Float Trips

1. Bluestone Dam tailwaters access area to above Brooks Falls, approximately 4.5 miles
   Put-in: Access areas on both sides of river below Bluestone Dam.
   Take-out: Brooks Falls day-use access point, River Road, above Brooks Falls.

2. Below Sandstone Falls to Meadow Creek access area, approximately 4.5 miles
   Put-in: Sandstone Falls access area below Sandstone Falls on River Road.
   Take-out: Meadow Creek access area, Meadow Creek Road, off W.Va. Rt. 20, near the Rt. 20 intersection with Interstate 64.

3. Meadow Creek access area to Prince *(Expert boaters only),* approximately 5.0 miles
   Put-in: Meadow Creek access area (described above).
   Take-out: Prince access area, off W.Va. Rt. 41, and McKendree Road.

Note: This section contains some Class I and Class II rapids that many fishermen might find too challenging. If you doubt your abilities to handle such water, stick to fishing this area from the bank or by wading selected sections.

This section of the New may be one of the top warm water fisheries in the entire country. Studies by the West Virginia Department of Nat-

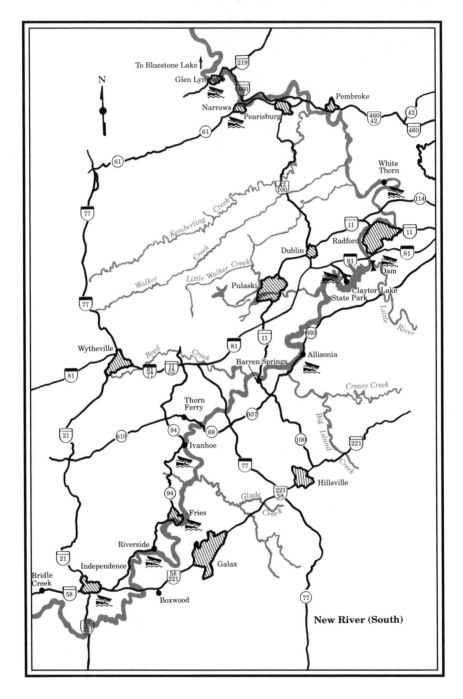

To Bluestone Lake
Glen Lyn
N
Narrows
Pearisburg
Pembroke
White Thorn
Radford
Dublin
Pulaski
Dam
Claytor Lake State Park
Wytheville
Barren Springs
Allisonia
Thorn Ferry
Ivanhoe
Fries
Hillsville
Riverside
Independence
Galax
Bridle Creek
Boxwood

New River (South)

ural Resources show that nearly every species of warm water gamefish found in the state can also be found in this section of the New.

This is also, without qualification, the most dangerous section of any river covered in the book. In pointing this out, I feel torn between an obligation to make this known to fishermen, while at the same time not wanting to discourage them from sampling this wonderful fishing opportunity.

Many areas within this section are completely safe to fish if normal precautions are taken. However, if you don't feel comfortable boating the river, you should note that wading and bank fishermen do very well, and there are many, many places where wading and/or bank fishing are possible.

The most heavily fished area is just below Bluestone Dam at Hinton. This tailrace area is controlled by the amount of water being released by the dam. The ideal level for wading is a flow of between one and three cubic feet per second; above three cubic feet per second the current gets too heavy for wading. To check the flow, contact the U.S. Army Corps of Engineers office at Hinton.

The area below the dam is great for the wading fisherman, and during normal flows you can fish most of the area easily. The habitat is a combination of riffles, cuts, drop-offs, and pools that are perfect for almost all species.

Smallmouth bass, channel cats, white bass, carp, and several species of panfish are the most frequent catches, but other species, such as flathead catfish, white/striped bass hybrids, spotted bass, and muskies, have also been taken.

During the warm weather months, wading fishermen seem to prefer live bait, drifted with the current. Hellgramites are the overwhelming choice of most anglers, and many bait shops in the area offer them for sale.

As the river heads down toward Sandstone Falls, there are several long deep pools that appear to be perfect habitat for bigger game—muskies and flathead catfish—and the species that prefer slow-moving water, like largemouth bass and crappies. River Road parallels the river for most of the way from W.Va. Rt. 3 to Sandstone Falls, and you can easily spot sections that you might want to fish.

The areas below Brooks Falls and above Sandstone Falls offer excellent wading opportunities.

The area below Sandstone Falls down to Meadow Creek is my favorite part of the river. This section offers the combination of long, deep pools and small drop-offs and riffles that is simply perfect habitat for

Outdoors writer Gerald Almy lands a 5½-pound smallmouth. Photo courtesy Gerald Almy

river gamefish. It is not a particularly dangerous section of river to boat if you are experienced, but, in saying this, I am reminded of tales of anglers drowning in the area over the past several years. Be careful and wear your PFD (personal flotation device). This is prime river fishing for the careful boater.

The area from Meadow Creek to Prince offers some exciting fishing, but is also rather challenging boating. The only reason I have included it is because so many anglers do choose to test the waters. In fact, many fish the entire stretch from below Sandstone Falls to Prince as one long float trip of about 10 miles.

My advice would be to break it up into two trips, and fish both sections more carefully, particularly the Sandstone Falls–to–Meadow Branch stretch. As mentioned before, the Meadow Creek–to–Prince run is for experienced boaters only. If you are a good canoeist, this can be very good water to fish. If not, stay out of this section of the river.

Wading and bank anglers will find some excellent opportunities in the Quinnimont and Prince areas. This is the best way to fish the area if you are uncomfortable about boating the section. You can also gain access to the river downstream from Prince, heading toward Thayer and Thurmond by following McKendree Road, off W.Va. Rt. 41 at Prince.

A few hardy anglers go deep into the New River Gorge in the Fayetteville area by following the C&O Railroad tracks that run along the river. This is beautiful country, and wild water fishing. It should be noted, however, that the tracks are used daily by trains and I'm not really clear if using the tracks is condoned by railroad officials. However, many anglers do take this route, and there is little doubt in my mind that the area has mind-boggling big fish potential.

EIGHTEEN

The Shenandoah River

The Shenandoah River is one of the most important rivers of this book, the reasons being that it offers many miles of prime fishing and boating opportunities, and it lies in a part of the country that is readily accessible to anglers living in metropolitan centers like Washington, Baltimore, and Richmond, and other large cities in the Middle Atlantic region.

One can't help but think of the important role the river has played in our country's history. It has been a part of our national heritage throughout the Revolutionary War, the War of 1812, and, of course, the Civil War.

The Shenandoah's main stem is formed from the confluence of the North and South forks at Front Royal, Virginia. Both forks of the river offer pretty good fishing opportunities, but the North Fork is considerably smaller and during the summer months becomes hard to boat—even with a canoe.

The upper part of the South Fork is nearly the same; for that reason, we will start with the lower section of the South Fork and then take the river downstream to its confluence with the Potomac at Harpers Ferry, West Virginia.

From my point of view, the best fishing on the river is from the Morgan Ford landing south of Front Royal, downstream through the remainder of the river in Virginia, and the twenty-mile section in West Virginia. The river widens and becomes more navigable, and the pools are deeper and hold better fish.

I've fished both the North and South forks, and have never had any trouble catching lots of bass, but they have been uniformly small. It's not difficult to catch a hundred or more smallmouths per day in many areas, and I've seen schools of small fish nearly fight over the opportunity to be the first one to eat a fly or lure. The river seems terribly overpopulated with small fish; perhaps the forage base is insufficient for the number of fish in the river.

Virginia is experimenting with various slot limits (most slots protect fish within a given size range, e.g., 11-14 inches; fish not in this slot are legal to harvest) and other measures to help reduce the percentage of small bass, but for now I would consider the North and South forks excellent places for lots of action, but poor choices if you are after quality fish.

The main stem from Morgan Ford down is another matter. The fish are in better shape, anglers have an excellent chance of landing smallmouths in the four-pound and larger range, and the area also holds a surprising number of largemouth bass. This is a nice fishing opportunity, particularly for float fishermen.

The Shenandoah is basically a float-fishing river. There are a few places where you can launch a properly rigged riverboat and motor for some distance when the water is up slightly, but, for the most part, you will be better off planning a float trip to fish this river.

The Shenandoah would be an even better river if it had not been plagued over the years by different environmental problems whose history goes back many years.

The latest incident occurred during the summer of 1989 when it was discovered that PCBs—polychlorinated biphenyls—were present in the river from Front Royal downstream to the Potomac.

PCBs are a serious matter, as witness the infamous Love Canal situation in New York and other similar disasters throughout the country.

Both largemouth (top) and smallmouth bass are taken in the Berryville area.

At the time of this writing, many questions on the PCB issue remain unanswered. The fact that PCBs are present in the fish of the river is a documented fact. The levels and the effect of the levels on humans seems to remain in doubt.

Both Virginia and West Virginia have conducted studies of the river fish, both forage fish and gamefish. The PCBs are present in the fish, but the effects on humans who consume such fish is a matter of some debate.

As a very interested observer on this tragic case, I would recommend the following: Continue to fish the river downstream from Front Royal, but do not eat any fish from the river. It may or may not (depending on which expert you believe) be unsafe to eat the occasional fish from the river, but I would not risk it.

For those of you who consider a fish or two for the table to be an integral part of the overall fishing experience, I would recommend fishing another river. But if you normally release the fish you catch, this situation may not turn out to be as bad as you might think.

At this time it would appear to me that two things are likely to happen over the next few years: First, I think the fishing pressure on the river will drop dramatically. Many if not most of the anglers fishing the river were folks hoping to take home a fish or two for dinner. Second, with practically none of the fish being killed for eating, the result will be a catch-and-return fishery much like the trout streams managed under such regulations.

The above is in no way meant to minimize the consequences of the PCBs in the river. This is indeed an important and serious matter with ramifications that go well beyond the potential loss of sportfishing opportunities. But, unfortunately, this is not an incident without precedent. Other rivers have suffered similar pollution, and fishing continued with the stipulation that no fish be killed for the table. The Housatonic River in Connecticut comes to mind. The trout from this river were declared unfit for human consumption after PCBs found their way into the river. The resulting fishery under the no-kill regulations has become nationally famous.

Certainly, no angler would wish pollution such as this upon any river or stream. But life goes on, and anglers can continue to fish the Shenandoah below Front Royal. But until you learn otherwise from competent authorities, I would strongly suggest that you refrain from eating any fish taken from the river beginning at Front Royal, downstream to the confluence with the Potomac.

GAMEFISH OF THE SHENANDOAH

Smallmouth Bass

The Shenandoah is best known as a smallmouth stream. The North Fork, the South Fork, and the main stem are all excellent smallmouth waters. I've spent the most time fishing the main stem, but have also enjoyed excellent success on the North and South forks.

My experiences on these two branches, which parallel experiences of friends, indicate that while you nearly always catch lots of small-mouths, the average size will usually be quite small—far smaller, in my experience, than the average size of fish taken from the other rivers.

By now, fans of the Shenandoah are probably gnashing their teeth with resentment; but rest assured I don't mean to discourage anyone from fishing this splendid river, but only to point out that you can reasonably expect to catch a lot of bass while floating the North Fork, South Fork, or upper main stem, and that's always a primary reason to fish any river. However, your chances of catching a lunker smallmouth aren't as good as they would be on some of the other rivers.

The West Virginia Department of Natural Resources conducted an interesting survey of the river during 1985. This study, which will also be referred to in the discussions of the other river species, polled fishermen on the twenty-mile section of the river flowing through West Virginia to determine their success, and to discover the species the fishermen were hoping to catch.

The survey provided a lot of interesting data. The results show that 45 percent of the 19,493 anglers surveyed indicated that they were fishing for mixed species (bass, catfish, panfish) and 38 percent were after bass specifically. Also interesting was the fact that smallmouth bass were by far the most frequently caught species, making up 47 percent of the total catch.

It was particularly notable, in light of the PCB problem currently affecting the river, that more than 75 percent of the smallmouth bass caught were released by fishermen. It should be noticed, however, that only 11 percent of the smallmouth bass over fourteen inches were released.

Most of my bass fishing on the Shenandoah has been done with artificial lures and flies, but if you wanted to catch a big smallmouth in the river during a summer float trip, you should have a couple of dozen stonecats to use as bait. The Shenandoah is an excellent stonecat river, containing the right type of aquatic vegetation for the little catfish to

Fly casting to rising fish on the South Fork of the Shenandoah River.

live in, and the chances of hooking a big bass would increase dramatically if you used the little catfish for bait.

During the fall I've enjoyed excellent fishing with surface lures. Tiny Torpedos, Devil's Horses, and fly rod popping bugs have provided lots of action, with many fish exceeding fourteen inches in length.

Largemouth Bass

The Shenandoah may not look like a largemouth river, but it contains an excellent population of the fish. I've caught many nice largemouths in the Berryville, Virginia, area and in the Big Eddy section in West Virginia. The largemouths, as usual, tend to hang near some shoreline cover, and jigs and pork rind have been the best producers for me.

Catfish

The West Virginia survey shows that channel cats are very popular with anglers on the river, making up 11 percent of the overall catch.

*Pan-sized catfish were a favorite at-
traction for Shenandoah anglers before the PCB problems.*

As is the case in all of the rivers, most catfishermen tend to favor cut bait and chicken livers as bait, but anglers who identified themselves as going after mixed species catch lots of cats on night crawlers and worms.

With the PCB problem, I would think that catfish would be particularly dangerous table fare, since they feed directly on the bottom, often on items lower in the food chain.

Panfish
Redbreast sunfish are very common throughout the river, and the West Virginia survey showed that sunfish—redbreast, bluegill, and pumpkinseed—were by far the most frequently harvested of the species taken home for the frying pan.

Rock bass are also common in certain sections and I've caught a few crappies from the Berryville, Virginia, section.

Muskie
Muskies have been stocked in the West Virginia section for many years now, and occasionally turn up in anglers' catches. One October I had a

couple of them located and managed to hook one particular fish several times. When winter fell, the score was Muskie 3, Anderson 0, and the fish was not there the following spring (at least I couldn't get it to hit again).

Big lures are usually the ticket for muskies and, for what it is worth, the fish I hooked showed a particular fondness for Storm Wiggle Wart crankbait lures in crawfish color.

Selected Sections of the River

Section I: South Branch. Bentonville to Front Royal
Suggested Float Trips

1. Bentonville to Karo, approximately 8 miles
   Put-in: Bentonville landing, County Rt. 613, off US Rt. 340, west of town of Bentonville.
   Take-out: Karo landing, County Rt. 623, north of Limeton.

2. Karo to Front Royal, approximately 6 miles
   Put-in: Karo landing (described above).
   Take-out: Front Royal landing, off US Rt. 340, south end of Front Royal.

Section II. Morgan Ford to Va. Rt. 7 east of Berryville
Suggested Float Trips

1. Morgan Ford to US Rt. 50, approximately 11 miles
   Put-in: Morgan Ford landing, County Rt. 624 south of Front Royal.
   Take-out: US Rt. 50 bridge, east of Winchester, Va.

2. US Rt. 50 to Locke landing, approximately 9 miles
   Put-in: US Rt. 50 (described above).
   Take-out: Locke landing, County Rt. 608, near Berryville, Va.

3. Locke landing to US Rt. 7, approximately 6 miles
   Put-in: Locke landing (described above).
   Take-out: US Rt. 7 bridge east of Berryville, Va.

Section III. US Rt. 7 to Millville, W. Va.
Suggested Float Trips

1. US Rt. 7 bridge to Shannondale Ferry, approximately 8 miles
   Put-in: US Rt. 7 bridge (described above).

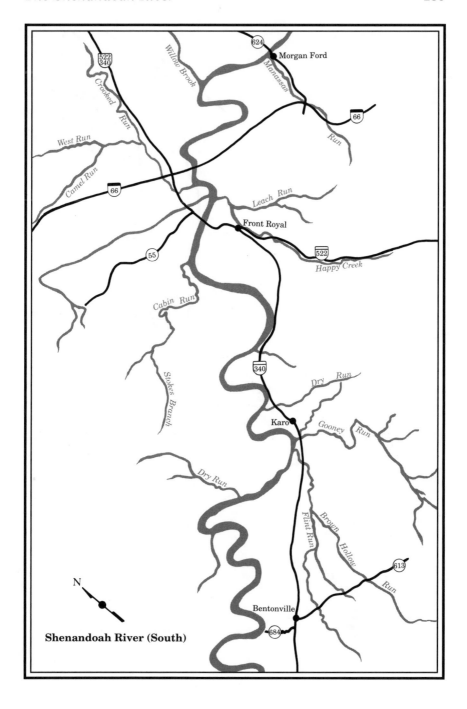

Shenandoah River (South)

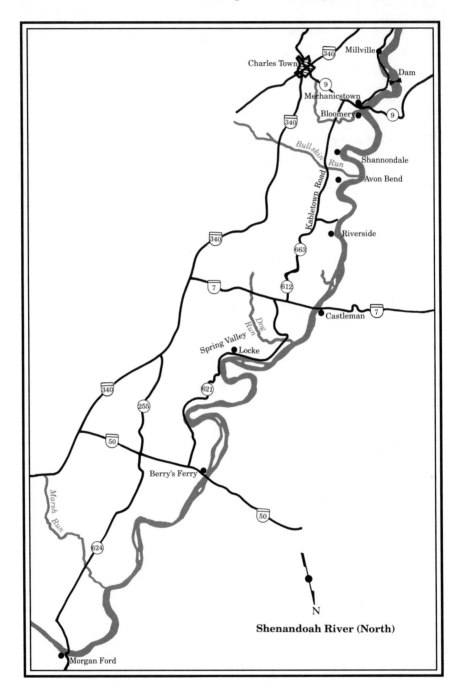

Shenandoah River (North)

Take-out: Shannondale Ferry access, off Kabletown Road, W. Va. Rt. 9, east of Charles Town, W. Va.

2. Shannondale Ferry to W. Va. Rt. 9 bridge, Bloomery, approximately 4 miles
   Put-in: Shannondale ferry (described above).
   Take-out: W. Va. Rt. 9 bridge access, Bloomery, W. Va.

3. W. Va. Rt. 9 bridge, Bloomery, to Millville ramp, approximately 2 miles
   Put-in: W. Va. Rt. 9 Bloomery bridge access (described above).
   Take-out: Millville ramp, Bloomery Road, north of W. Va. Rt. 9.

The above list gives the angler a variety of choices. Almost without exception, the Shenandoah is a float-fishing river. The float above Front Royal, from Bentonville to the Karo ramp, is a nice fishermen's float.

Most of the floats from Morgan Ford downstream are the same— relatively flat water interspersed with the occasional riffles that are easily navigated with the river at normal levels.

The Millville ramp is above the dam at Millville and is one of the few places where you can launch your riverboat and motor successfully. In this case you must motor upstream away from the dam toward the W. Va. Rt. 9 bridge at Bloomery. This area is locally called the Big Eddy and offers some of the best-looking water on the river.

Below the Millville dam, the river changes quite rapidly as it approaches the Potomac, and traverses some white water areas that are quite popular with canoeists when the flow level is right. This area can be fished, but I wouldn't recommend that the average boater try to fish it from a boat. Some of it can be waded and fished, but be forewarned that the footing is tricky and this water can be treacherous when the flow is up in the spring and early summer.

The Shenandoah is one of our most important rivers. Every smallmouth fisherman should fish the river as often as possible and many do just that.

The situation with the PCBs casts a terrible shadow over the fishing future on the river. But even if our worst fears are proven correct, we should still be able to enjoy the fishing on a catch-and-return basis.

NINETEEN

The South Branch of the Potomac River

This chapter is unique in that a major branch of a river is treated as a separate entity. The South Branch rates such coverage because of the outstanding fishing opportunity it provides fishermen and the importance of the river in the overall scheme of fishing within the mid-Atlantic region.

The South Branch is formed by the junction of the North and South forks near Petersburg, West Virginia; it then travels some forty-eight miles to its confluence with the North Branch, approximately eighteen miles southeast of Cumberland, Maryland.

The South Branch provides excellent fishing from Petersburg to its confluence with the North Branch. In addition, it offers some of the most majestic scenery to be found in this part of the nation.

The most famous section of the river is probably the Trough, which is a six-mile cut through the mountains interlaced with impressive boulders and underwater rock formations.

The now-famous flood of November 1985 left its mark: In some cases the river actually changed course. And throughout the upper river, the power of the flood was in evidence with millions of dollars' worth of property lost to the raging waters.

As time goes on, the river continues to heal from the scouring flood, but some parts of it were changed forever. Pools filled with silt and no longer offer attractive habitat for gamefish; and sections that may have been heavily populated with smallmouths may now hold only sunfish and carp.

The lasting damage to the river is far more evident in the upper sections. The lower river, from Romney, West Virginia, down, was less affected and is very much as it was before the flood.

Several local anglers feel that the river is not as productive now as before the flood, and that's probably the case. But nature has her own way of dealing with such matters, and over the course of time the South Branch will continue to improve and recover. As this chapter is written, the lower river is still an excellent fishery and will continue to be one of the best smallmouth rivers in the region, offering a fishing opportunity that is unique to the rivers in this book in terms of geography and scenery.

GAMEFISH OF THE SOUTH BRANCH

Smallmouth Bass

The South Branch is best known for the nine-pound, twelve-ounce smallmouth taken from its waters in 1971. This fish, which has been mentioned in other chapters, ranks as one of the most important records in freshwater fishing, especially when one considers the odds of a smallmouth bass reaching such size in so small a river.

The chances of catching such a fish in any river are indeed slim, but the South Branch does produce excellent fishing for two- and three-pound smallmouths with occasional fish reaching even greater weights.

In 1988, the West Virginia Department of Natural Resources enacted special catch-and-return regulations on two sections of the South Branch and the new rules will be of interest to any angler visiting the river. When fishing the two sections, anglers will be required to return all black bass (largemouth and smallmouth) to the water immediately. No bass are allowed in an angler's possession.

The first section is in Hardy County from the Petersburg Gap bridge downstream to the Fisher bridge, a distance of approximately eight miles. The second section is in Hampshire County, from the Romney bridge downstream to the W. Va. Rt. 28 bridge, a distance of approximately 9.5 miles.

This is the state's first experiment in catch-and-return regulations for a warm water fishery. The policy will be in effect until December 31, 1993; at that time the results of the restriction will be evaluated and, if warranted, the Hardy County site may become a permanent catch-and-return section.

Most South Branch fishermen float the river in canoes and small johnboats. A limited number of lures are needed. Small crankbaits, surface lures, and curlytail grubs are usually good choices.

The South Branch is an excellent hellgramite river, and if you are a live bait angler, a supply of hellgramites would be a good idea. I've

David Lindsay with his incredible state record small-mouth that weighed 9 pounds 12 ounces and was 24¼ inches long. Photo courtesy Mike Sawyers

also done well on various fly rod poppers. During the summer, evening hatches of mayflies and caddis flies will often provide excellent dry fly action.

Largemouth Bass

An interesting sidebar on the river is that, since the flood of November 1985, the number of largemouth bass has increased dramatically. Gerald Lewis, the West Virginia DNR biologist in charge of the river, has conducted studies that document this increase, and says that many pools that were once devoid of largemouths now contain far more largemouths than smallmouths.

This increase may be a result of fish washed into the river by the flood, and may reflect a change in habitat caused by the flood. For my money, though, it is not necessarily a change for the better. The smallmouth is a more fitting fish for this type of water and hopefully the South Branch will remain, first and foremost, a smallmouth river.

Catfish

Most of the South Branch is good catfish water. The better catfish section seems to be the lower part of the river. The cats usually take up residence in the deeper pools, and chicken and groundhog (woodchuck) livers are the favored baits.

Carp
I've never caught a carp from the river, and have never met anyone fishing specifically for carp, but the fish are there. Many times on float trips we've drifted over pods of big carp, some of which appeared to weigh fifteen pounds or more. The usual carp baits—doughballs and worms—would probably take lots of carp from the bigger pools.

Panfish
Redbreast sunfish, rock bass, and bluegills are quite abundant in the South Branch. Rock bass are one of the more frequent catches and are often taken when the angler is fishing for smallmouths, since they prefer similar habitats. Redbreast sunfish are quite common throughout the river and seem particularly abundant in the lower float trip areas. Small artificial lures used for smallmouths will also take the panfish; in fact, when using hellgramites, you will often have a hard time keeping the panfish off long enough for a smallmouth to get a shot at your bait.

ACCESS TO THE RIVER

Public access to the South Branch is excellent. This is a float trip river and the access points are mostly carry-in points that the state either owns or leases.

The following float trips are listed in the West Virginia DNR fishing regulations guidebook that is distributed with the licenses and are good starting points for planning a South Branch trip.

Put-in	Take-Out	Mileage
Petersburg bridge	Petersburg Gap	3.0
Petersburg Gap	Fisher bridge	8.0
Fisher bridge	Old Fields bridge	4.5
Old Fields bridge	Trough entrance	5.0
Trough entrance	Glebe access	6.25
Hampshire Park	Romney bridge	3.25
Romney bridge	Wapocomo	5.0
Wapocomo	Grace (Blue Beach bridge)	5.0
Grace	Millesons Mill	7.25
Millesons Mill	New Bridge	2.5
New Bridge	Blue Ford	4.5
Blue Ford	Indian Rock	4.0
Indian Rock	Mouth	4.5

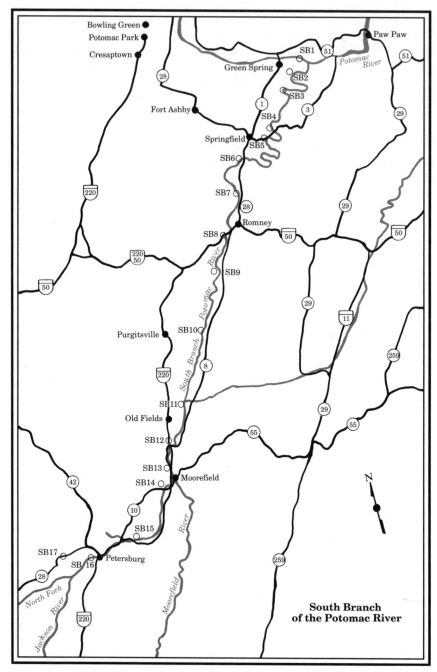

Bowling Green
Potomac Park
Cresaptown
Paw Paw
SB1 51
51
Potomac River
28
Green Spring
SB2
SB3
29
1
3
Fort Ashby
SB4
Springfield
SB5
SB6
220
SB7
28
29
Romney
SB8
50
50
50
SB9
220
50
29
50
220
50
SB10
11
Purgitsville
8
259
220
SB11
29
Old Fields
SB12
55
55
SB13
42
SB14 Moorefield
N
10
259
SB15
SB17
Petersburg
SB16
28
North Fork
Jackson River
220
Moorefield River

**South Branch
of the Potomac River**

South Branch Potomac River

(See pages 167 and 168 for SB insets.)

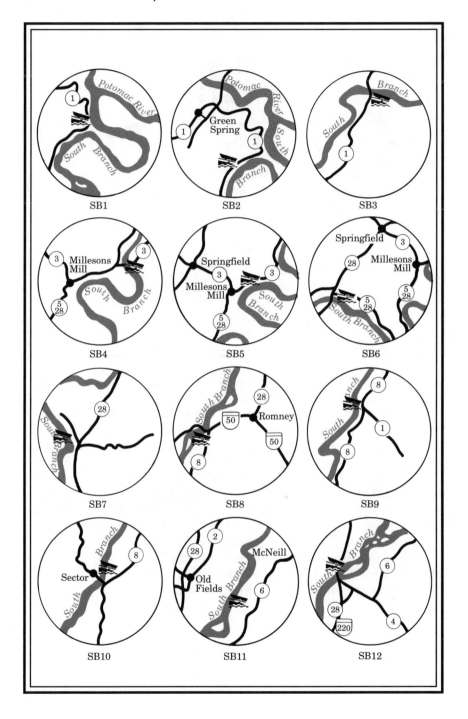

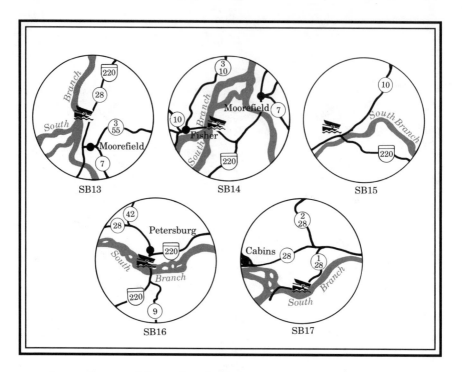

As can be noted from the above list, there are many different float trip possibilities of varying lengths.

For the most part, the South Branch is a gentle river that can be boated by a reasonably competent paddler, but the situation changes during high waters after rains, and during cold weather (because of the danger of hypothermia). The Trough section is an interesting ride and in the spring and summer at normal river flows it can be boated rather easily. But there is a drop-off at the head of the Trough that can spill you if you aren't careful. The other sections offer various riffles and ledges that must be navigated, but if you are experienced at handling a canoe or johnboat, you should manage easily.

The South Branch offers one of the finest fishing experiences to be found in the mid-Atlantic and is highly recommended if you enjoy quality smallmouth fishing in a mountainous setting.

TWENTY

The Greenbrier River

Like most of the rivers in the book, the Greenbrier has its beginning as a mountain brook, in the mountains of northern Pocahontas County; its two forks, the East and West, join near the town of Durbin.

The Greenbrier is a small river but, despite its diminutive size, rates as one of the better smallmouth bass rivers in the mid-Atlantic region. This is a float trip and wade-fishing river, although during the late summer and fall months, some of the upper sections we will cover may be rather shallow.

Floating the Greenbrier is an enjoyable fishing adventure, and, though the Greenbrier can't be expected to compete with large rivers such as the brawling New in terms of trophy fish potential, citation records show that the river does grow a somewhat surprising number of trophy-sized smallmouths, flathead catfish, and walleyes.

GAMEFISH OF THE GREENBRIER

Smallmouth Bass

Smallmouths are the featured attraction on the river, and for most anglers quantity rather than quality is the reward. A little river like the Greenbrier can't be expected to produce big smallmouths at the rate that bigger rivers can, but anglers enjoy the scenic beauty of the Greenbrier and the large numbers of bass that a typical float trip can produce.

The Greenbrier is a relatively fertile river, with an excellent forage base of aquatic insects and small baitfish. Studies by fisheries biologists show that it is one of the few rivers in the state that have remained relatively pollution free. Studies also show that smallmouths make up approximately 30 percent of the total population, which is quite high—particularly in a river with the population diversity of the Greenbrier.

Although most of the smallmouths taken are on the small side, the river does have trophy smallmouth potential. Studies of citation rec-

169

ords show that the river consistently produces citation-sized small-mouths on a yearly basis.

Largemouth and Spotted Bass
Largemouth and spotted bass are found in the river, particularly in the deeper pools in the lower section. Both species are caught on an irregular basis, and many anglers confuse the spotted bass with the more common smallmouth.

Walleye
Although walleyes aren't one of the more frequently caught of the Greenbrier gamefish, the river does have a stable, self-sustaining population of this fine species. Some grow quite large, like the fourteen-pound, six-ounce monster caught by Elmer Reed of Alderson in February 1984. That was a very big walleye.

The walleyes are usually found in the deeper pools, and are frequently caught in the cool-weather months from November through March. Not many anglers catch them regularly, but big fish are there if you know the proper techniques.

Float trippers will often encounter walleyes on the Greenbrier.

Catfish

Both channel catfish and big flatheads are found in the river. Once again, the lower section in the deeper pools is the habitat to try for them.

The Greenbrier often ranks second behind the New in trophy flathead citations, which is quite an accomplishment when you consider all the top catfish waters in the state.

Carp

According to studies by the West Virginia biologists, carp aren't abundant in the Greenbrier, but they can be found in certain areas. Biologist Jim Reed said that some of the carp are very big—twenty pounds and over—which would present an interesting challenge in such small water.

Panfish

The Greenbrier supports an excellent panfish population. Rock bass are the most common panfish, as is usually the case in smallmouth

Angler fishing through a carpet of leaves in October.

rivers. Other frequently caught panfish include green sunfish, longear sunfish, and bluegill. Float fishermen after smallmouths will have many encounters with the panfish during most trips.

ACCESS TO THE GREENBRIER

Access to the river is adequate. Most of the access points are at bridges over the river. But anglers seem not to mind the access problems, because the river remains one of the most popular float-fishing rivers in the state.

There are many different float trip possibilities, as you can see from the following list.

Suggested Float Trips

1. Denmar to Renick, approximately 11.5 miles
   Put-in: Town of Denmar off US Rt. 219.
   Take-out: Town of Renick, County Rt. 11 off US Rt. 219.

2. Renick to Anthony, approximately 9.5 miles
   Put-in: Town of Renick (described above).
   Take-out: Town of Anthony, County Rt. 21/2 off US Rt. 219.

3. Anthony to Caldwell, approximately 11 miles
   Put-in: Anthony (described above).
   Take-out: Interstate Rt. 64 bridge near Caldwell.

4. Caldwell to Ronceverte
   Put-in: Caldwell (described above).
   Take-out: Ronceverte, US Rt. 219 bridge in City Park.

5. Fort Spring to Alderson, approximately 6 miles
   Put-in: Town of Fort Spring off W. Va. Rt. 63.
   Take-out: Town of Alderson, off W. Va. Rt. 3.
   Note: This float contains some Class I or II rapids (depending on flow level) and is recommended only for experienced boaters.

6. Alderson to Pence Springs, approximately 4.5 miles
   Put-in: Town of Alderson off W. Va. Rt. 3.
   Take-out: Pence Springs, W. Va. Rt. 3 at its intersection with County Rt. 15.

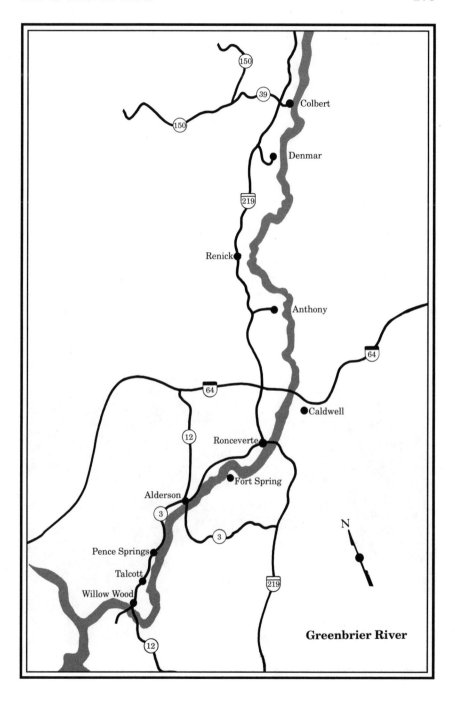

Greenbrier River

7. Pence Springs to Talcott, approximately 4.5 miles
   Put-in: Pence Springs (described above).
   Take-out: Talcott, off County Rt. 17.

8. Talcott to Willow Wood, approximately 10 miles
   Put-in: Talcott (described above).
   Take-out: Willow Wood, off W. Va. Rt. 3.
   Note: This section requires two short portages around falls. Be careful.

This river offers a nice variety of float-fishing trips, and an excellent opportunity to enjoy what I call the complete river fishing experience. One comment I have to add, however, is that some of this experience is being diminished by the large number of summer homes and fishing shanties that are springing up along the river. This is especially true from Alderson downstream to Willow Wood.

Anglers should note that this river can sometimes get quite shallow in the upper sections, even for float tripping in shallow-draft canoes. The particularly dry summer of 1988 caused the water level during early fall of that year to be too low for floating as far down-

The Greenbrier runs through gentle scenic country that most anglers will enjoy.

stream as Alderson. A float trip in late May or June may be the best bet for the upper sections of the river.

The Greenbrier should be on every smallmouth fisherman's list of waters to test. It is a beautiful mountain river with a proven track record of producing smallmouth bass and the occasional walleye in sizes to suit the most avid trophy fisherman.